1000 Sadie Sink Facts

Mera Wolfe

Other Books By Mera Wolfe

1000 Millie Bobby Brown Facts

-

1000 All New Millie Bobby Brown Facts

-

1000 Friends Facts

-

1000 Finn Wolfhard Facts

-

1000 Bella Ramsey Facts

-

1000 Billie Eilish Facts

-

1000 Selena Gomez Facts

-

1000 Ariana Grande Facts

Contents

INTRODUCTION

1000 Sadie Sink Facts contains 1000 facts about this acting superstar.

Facts about Stranger Things, Fear Street, The Whale, Annie, The Audience, Broadway, fashion, All Too Well: A Short Film, Taylor Swift, family, likes & dislikes, food, career, background, lifestyle, friends, quotes, awards, beauty products, and so much more all awaits in 1000 Sadie Sink Facts.

1000 SADIE SINK FACTS

(1) Sadie Sink was born in Brenham, Texas, on 16 April 2002.

(2) Sadie's full name is Sadie Elizabeth Sink.

(3) Brenham is a city in east-central Texas in Washington County, United States, with a population of 17,369 according to the 2020 U.S. census.

(4) Sadie's parents are Casey Adam Sink (football coach) and Lori Elizabeth Sink (mathematics teacher).

(5) Sadie has three older brothers and one younger sister.

(6) Sadie's brothers are named Mitchell, Spencer, and Caleb.

(7) Sadie's sister is Jaci Joy AKA Jacey.

(8) Sadie has blue eyes.

(9) Sadie is 5'3 in height.

(10) Sadie's red hair is completely natural.

(11) At the time of writing, Sadie has nearly 27 million followers on Instagram.

(12) Sadie was about seven when she started acting and performing for fun.

(13) When Sadie started acting and performing as a kid, her parents had to take her to Houston for her performing classes.

(14) Sadie is of English, Irish and German descent.

(15) Sadie's favourite food is pasta.

(16) One of Sadie's early roles was as Baby Angel Shirley in The Best Christmas Pageant Ever. This was a community theater production. Sadie had one line!

(17) Sadie appeared in a stage version of White Christmas in 2011.

(18) When she was a kid, Sadie's family moved from Texas to New Jersey to help her acting career. They wanted to be closer to New York.

(19) An obsession with Disney's High School Musical led Sadie to take acting classes in community theatre and at the age of eleven a Broadway audition landed her a role in the revival of Annie.

(20) Sadie's television roles include Blue Bloods and The Americans and she featured in eleven episodes of the thriller series American Odyssey.

(21) Sadie had a small role in the 2016 film Chuck, which starred Liev Schreiber and told the story of boxer Chuck Wepner.

(22) Sadie appeared in the 2017 film The Glass Castle, which starred Brie Larson and Woody Harrelson.

(23) Sadie is a vegan.

(24) Sadie said watching the 2008 documentary film Food Inc was one of the things that made her stop eating meat. Food

Inc offers a grim look at the reality of the food and farming industry in America. Sadie said that co-star Woody Harrelson was also an influence on going vegan.

(25) Sadie was a vegetarian for a time before she became a vegan.

(26) Sadie became a vegan when she was fourteen.

(27) Sadie said that when she became a vegetarian no one though she would last a week so this made her determined to prove everyone wrong.

(28) Sadie said it was a bit tricky becoming a vegan because her family in Texas were all big meat eaters.

(29) Sadie has freckles.

(30) Sadie's favourite band are Foo Fighters.

(31) Stranger Things 2 added another girl to the gang of younger characters. The new character was Maxine 'Max' Mayfield - a tomboy from California who has moved to Hawkins and attracted the curiosity and early romantic emotions of Lucas and Dustin. It was Sadie who won this coveted role.

(32) Sadie said she had five callbacks during her audition process before she was cast as Maxine Mayfield in Stranger Things 2. A callback means that the director would like to see an actor again - perhaps to hear them read from the script or see them perform a scene next to another actor. Getting a callback doesn't automatically mean you have a part fin the bag but if you keep getting called back this is obviously a good sign because it means they want to see you again.

(33) Maxine Mayfield - known as Max - is a girl who arrives in Hawkins and eventually becomes friends with the boys - especially Lucas. She attracts their attention when she beats some of Dustin's high scores at the arcade. Max is a skateboarding tomboy with a somewhat cynical wit. Her home life is not terribly enviable as she has to live with her overbearing and thuggish older step-brother Billy. Max is told the secrets of Hawkins by Lucas and although she (understandably) doesn't believe him at first she later experiences the dimensional monster mayhem of Hawkins for herself and accepts that Lucas was telling the truth.

(34) When she did her auditions for the part of Max, Sadie had to read some scenes with Caleb McLaughlin and Gaten Matarazzo. They obviously needed to see if she had good chemistry with the other kids.

(35) Sadie had to do some skateboarding training in preparation for her part as Max.

(36) Because the character of Max is supposed to be from California, Sadie also had to have a little bit of fake-tan applied to make it look as if she'd recently got plenty of sun.

(37) Sadie found it quite funny that her character in Stranger Things was supposed to be from California because in real life she considers sunshine to be one of her deadliest enemies.

(38) Although the show Stranger Things is set in Indiana it is filmed just outside of Atlanta in Georgia.

(39) Sadie said she turned off her social media notifications when she was cast in Stranger Things 2. She found the imminent prospect of overnight fame surreal.

(40) Sadie enjoys a matcha latte. Matcha latte is a beverage that originates from Japan. It's made from finely ground green tea leaves that are mixed with steamed milk.

(41) Sadie said that the first wage packet she got for acting was spent on a laptop.

(42) Sadie has appeared in other horror roles while playing Max Mayfield.

She was in Fear Street Part One: 1994, Fear Street Part Two: 1978, Fear Street Part Three: 1666 and Eli. The Fear street films generally got good reviews but Eli did't fare so well. Fear Street Part One: 1994 is a 2021 horror film directed by Leigh Janiak. It is based on the Fear Street book series by R.L. Stine. The film is set in the fictional town of Shadyside, Ohio, and follows a group of teenagers who must uncover the dark secrets behind their town's history as they are haunted by a vengeful killer.

Fear Street Part Two: 1978 is the second installment in the Fear Street film trilogy on Netflix. It was released on July 9, 2021. The movie serves as a prequel to Fear Street Part One: 1994 and delves deeper into the cursed town of Shadyside.

Fear Street Part Three: 1666 is the final installment in the Fear Street trilogy directed by Leigh Janiak. This horror film serves as a prequel to the previous two films, Fear Street Part One: 1994 and Fear Street Part Two: 1978. The story takes place in the fictional town of Shadyside, with the narrative alternating between 1666 and the previous time periods. It explores the origins of the curse that has plagued the town for centuries. In this final chapter, the audience is transported back to the year 1666 and introduced to the residents of Union, which later became Shadyside.

(43) Eli is a 2019 American horror film directed by Ciarán Foy and written by David Chirchirillo, Ian Goldberg, and Richard Naing. The movie stars Charlie Shotwell as Eli, a young boy suffering from a debilitating illness, and Lili Taylor and Kelly Reilly as his parents. The story revolves around Eli, who is sent to a secluded clinic by his parents in hopes of finding a cure for his rare autoimmune disorder. However, as he undergoes treatment, Eli starts experiencing supernatural events and encounters eerie figures within the clinic's walls. He becomes determined to uncover the dark secrets behind the facility and discover the truth about his illness. Sadie plays a teenage girl in the film who helps Eli.

(44) Sadie's most prestigious role came in the 2022 Darren Aronofsky film The Whale. The Whale is based on the play of the same name by Samuel D. Hunter, which premiered off-Broadway in 2012. The film stars Brendan Fraser in the lead role and tells the story of Charlie, a 600-pound recluse who is literally trying to eat himself to death. In the film Sadie plays Charlie's estranged teenage daughter Ellie. Sadie won a lot of plaudits for her acting in this film.

(45) The younger version of Ellie you see in The Whale was played by Sadie's younger sister Jacey.

(46) Sadie said she hadn't seen any Brendan Fraser films until she was cast as his daughter in The Whale. Said said she then watched ALL of them after she was cast.

(47) Sadie said the toughest thing about joining the cast of Stranger Things was having to do photo-shoots, press tours, and interviews. All this stuff was new to her.

(48) Sadie's favourite colour is yellow.

(49) Sadie appeared in the sitcom Unbreakable Kimmy Schmidt. This was before Stranger Things.

(50) Maxine Mayfield in Stranger Things has a Madrid Skateboard. This is the same brand that Marty McFly has in Back to the Future.

(51) Sadie said that one thing you will always find in her fridge is Almond milk.

(52) The young Max you see during the flashback in the Stranger Things episode E Pluribus Unum is played by Sadie's sister Jacey.

(53) Sadie's favourite designer is Stella McCartney.

(54) Sadie said she binged Sex and the City to 'decompress' while shooting The Whale.

(55) Given that the children in the cast of Stranger Things were such a tight-knit bunch, the Duffers were a little worried about the introduction of another young actor into this group. These fears proved ungrounded and it quickly felt like both Max Mayfield and Sadie Sink had always been a part of Stranger Things.

(56) Sadie and Millie Bobby Brown got on so well they went on a family holiday together when shooting on season two of Stranger Things ended.

(57) Sadie has a phobia of spiders.

(58) Sadie said that one aspect of her Stranger Things character she doesn't share in real-life is an aptitude for video games. Max is something of an arcade fiend but Sadie said she

was hopeless at the games she played in the Palace Arcade set.

(59) Sadie said the smell of fake tanning lotion always reminds her of her early days on Stranger Things.

(60) Sadie said she doesn't adhere to any particular hair-care regimen.

(61) In three days, Stranger Things 2 had fifteen million viewers streaming it.

(62) There are a few mistakes in the arcade scenes in Stranger Things 2. The flat screen machines used in the show were not native to the cathode ray eighties and - as many pointed out - Max wouldn't have had enough characters available to enter 'MADMAX' on Dig Dug's high score gallery.

(63) Sadie won the rising star award at the 2022 SCAD Savannah Film Festival.

(64) Sadie starred in the Taylor Swift-directed music video "All Too Well: A Short Film."

(65) Sadie says it was a relief that Max didn't do much skateboarding in Stranger Things 3 as she had got quite rusty since her skateboarding training for Stranger Things 2.

(66) Sadie's hair is curly if left to its own devices.

(67) Sadie said she isn't really a fan of watching horror films but does like the more psychological ones like Get Out, Black Swan, and Us.

(68) Sadie had her long hair cut to shoulder length in 2023. She did this for her part in the film O'Dessa.

(69) Sadie said her ultimate dinner party guest would be Beyonce.

(70) Sadie said she enjoys watching YouTube videos.

(71) Sadie said it feels a bit surreal to watch herself in Stranger Things 2 now. "It's like this time capsule where there's this much younger, smaller me on Netflix."

(72) Caleb McLaughlin, Sadie, and Gaten Matarazzo all vaguely knew each other before Stranger Things because they had worked on Broadway and the stage and their paths had crossed.

(73) Sadie's favourite lipstick colour to wear is pink.

(74) The Michael Myers mask that Max wears at Halloween in Stranger Things 2 was surprisingly complicated to make because they didn't want it to look too professional. They wanted a mask that looked like a child or young teenager had made it themselves. Sadie had never actually heard of Michael Myers. The real Michael Myers in the original Halloween film wore a Captain Kirk Star Trek mask that the props people spray painted white. This is why John Carpenter has always joked that he owes his entire career to William Shatner. Look fast for a Jason Vorhees (the killer in the Friday the 13th films) in the background when the children are out trick or treating at Halloween in Stranger Things 2.

(75) Sadie said that one of her worst habits is biting her nails.

(76) Sadie said she doesn't have any social media apps on her phone.

(77) The Stranger Things youngsters were often seen at Six

flags amusement park in Georgia when early seasons of Stranger Things were in production. This theme park is only a twenty minute drive from Atlanta. Six flags amusement park now has a spooky Stranger Things maze.

(78) When they shot the Halloween scenes in Stranger Things 2 it was hot and humid in Georgia and the actors were quite sweaty so the production and makeup departments had to be very careful to hide this fact and depict an Autumnal aura.

(79) Sadie narrated the 2018 animal rights film Dominion, which is an exploration of modern-day animal agriculture.

(80) Apart from acting, Sadie has also trained in vocals and dance.

(81) For her Stranger Things auditions, one of the scenes Sadie had to do was the sequence where Billy is threatening to run the boys over in his car and Max is shouting at him.

(82) Sadie said that because she is surrounded by people all the time on film and TV sets she quite enjoys spending some time alone when she goes home.

(83) Sadie is a Global Ambassador for Armani Beauty.

(84) There was a rumpus in the media saying that Sadie felt uncomfortable in the Stranger Things 2 finale scene where Max and Lucas kiss but Sadie put out a statement saying this was not true.

(85) In 2018, for the animal rights documentary, Sadie was awarded the 2018 'Award of Excellence' for narration by the Hollywood International Independent Documentary Awards.

(86) The building used for the Starcourt Mall in Stranger Things 3 is Gwinnett Place Mall - located in the Pleasant Hill Road corridor of Duluth, Georgia. The mall opened in 1984 and has gone through various owners. The mall was largely derelict by the time that the Stranger Things production staff noticed it. The production team on Stranger Things built 40 storefronts with full interiors to create an authentic looking 80s mall.

(87) Sadie says that her attempt to take a few items from Starcourt Mall at the end of shooting didn't quite go according to plan. "That mall was huge, it's still nuts when I think about how big it was. When I first stepped onto that set I truly couldn't believe it. At the end of shooting, a few people went on some shopping sprees. Millie grabbed a shopping bag and went around the Gap and got a bunch of stuff. I picked out a few clothes, but I accidentally left them in my trailer and they never made it home."

(88) Netflix eventually dismantled the Starcourt Mall set - which felt like a shame. The reason behind this is presumed to be that they didn't want any intrepid fans to steal the props. The security on the site was also obviously costing them a lot of money.

(89) In 2018, Sadie participated for the first time at Paris Fashion Week in the Undercover Fall show.

(90) Sadie is a fan of Gucci.

(91) Sadie has been on the show Lip Sync Battle.

(92) Sadie was seen sporting flared jeans in 2023. Flares are finally back!

(93) Sadie was rumoured to be dating Joe Alywn's brother Patrick - after they were seen spending time together. This was never confirmed.

(94) Sadie is a very private person. Nothing is known about any relationships she might have had.

(95) Sadie was given three months off Stranger Things 4 to shoot The Whale. "The Duffers have always been so good because they know how much time the show takes and they still want us to build careers outside of it."

(96) Sadie said she wasn't told much about her character when she auditioned for Stranger Things.

(97) Sadie attended the Venice film festival in 2023.

(98) Sadie said she watches RuPaul's Drag Race.

(99) Sadie has modelled for Miu Miu.

(100) In Stranger Things 2, Max has a poster for the 1966 surf movie The Endless Summer in her room. The Endless Summer is a 1966 American surfing documentary film directed, produced, edited and narrated by Bruce Brown. Max seems to have the Australian poster for the film.

(101) The snowball scene in Stranger Things 2 scene was the first kiss both onscreen or in real life for both Sadie and Caleb McLaughlin.

(102) You can now buy a lifesize Sadie Sink cardboard cut-out.

(103) Sadie has a net worth of $1 million according to celebrity wealth sites. One would expect Stranger Things 5 to

increase this figure.

(104) Sadie said that her favorite fashion accessory is a pair of earrings.

(105) When they have to depict blood in a character's mouth (or even near their mouth) in Stranger Things, the makeup department uses a fake blood mixture that is made up of dried cranberries, black cherry Jell-O mix, Emergen-C powder, and some water. Emergen-C is a powdered vitamin supplement. The most important thing is that it has to be safe to go inside the actor's mouth.

(106) Sadie is a fan of the band Red Hot Chili Peppers.

(107) Kate Bush famously has an important sonic role in Stranger Things 4 as the musical guardian of Max Mayfield. When the producers decided that they wanted to use her song Running Up That Hill in the show they had to, as is custom, approach the artist to ask permission. Given that Kate Bush is rather reclusive and enigmatic and not known for wildly embracing the mainstream of popular culture (she once turned down an offer to sing the theme song for the Bond film Moonraker) it was certainly open to question whether or not contact would be made - let alone permission to use Running Up That Hill. To the delight of the Duffer Brothers though it transpired that Kate Bush was actually a big fan of Stranger Things and more than happy to let her song be used in the show.

(108) Sadie was allowed to take home and keep the Walkman that Max uses in Stranger Things 4.

(109) In the eighties it was common and standard for music albums to be released on cassette tapes and Walkmans (a

portable cassette player with earphones that allowed you to listen to music wherever you were) were popular. The first Walkman was released in 1979. Cassettes were of course easy to use and record on too. All music lovers in the 1980s would have had a big collection of cassette tapes on their shelf.

(110) Sadie had never actually heard of Kate Bush before she did Stranger Things 4.

(111) Sadie is a fan of Disneyland.

(112) Sadie said she once had an awful nightmare about being trapped in a volcano. Yikes!

(113) The film with the highest rating on Rotten Tomatoes that Sadie has been in is Fear Street Part Three: 1666. This is slightly surprising because one would presume that The Whale would have the highest RT score.

(114) Sadie was delighted to find a delicious vegan replacement 'chicken and waffles' (which she loved when she used to eat meat) at plant-based eatery Cafe Sunflower in Atlanta where Stranger Things is shot.

(115) Sadie said it took about two weeks for her to complete her auditions for Stranger Things 2.

(116) Sadie is a fan of Emma Stone.

(117) Sadie is a fan of the film Eternal Sunshine of the Spotless Mind.

(118) Sadie says that when she has a day off from acting she literally does nothing at all and just relaxes at home.

(119) 90% of the spores you see floating around in the Upside Down scenes in Stranger Things are digital.

(120) Sadie has 207 lines in Stranger Things 2 as Max. This gave her more lines in Stranger Things 2 than Natalia Dyer, Charlie Heaton, Noah Schnapp, and Joe Keery.

(121) Due to Covid restrictions - and doubtless time and expense - Dacre Montgomery shot his nightmare flashback cameo as Billy Hargrove in Stranger Things 4 in Australia and then it was spliced in with the episode Dear Billy. Despite his lack of interaction with the cast, Montgomery's usual intensity is plain to see and he more than makes the most of his chance to play Billy again. In the scene where Max has visions of her brother Billy in Dear Billy, Sadie shot her contribution to this scene an entire year after Dacre Montgomery!

(122) Sadie has attended events such as WE Day, a youth empowerment event that brings together celebrities and activists.

(123) Sadie said that when she's out and about in New York she is never bothered by the public.

(124) Sadie was nominated for a Saturn Award in 2022 for her role in Stranger Things.

(125) Sadie's favourite documentary is Blackfish. This film is about the treatment of orca whales at Seaworld.

(126) In her first week working on Stranger Things 2, Sadie went to an Adele concert with Millie Bobby Brown.

(127) The mall montage featuring Max and Eleven in Stranger

Things 3 was supposed to include a food feast and the girls getting their ears pierced but these scenes were not included in the end.

(128) Sadie has a pet dog.

(129) Sadie said she would love to work with the film directors Wes Anderson and Sofia Coppola.

(130) Sadie says she has something in common with her Stranger Things character in that neither wear much makeup.

(131) Sadie said she watched the first season of Stranger Things with her hands over her face because she found it too scary.

(132) Sadie said she loves the colour of 1980s fashions.

(133) Sadie is a fan of the 90s sitcom Seinfeld. She says the character of Elaine in that show is a bit of a fashion icon to her.

(134) The makeup department on Stranger Things 3 complained when the catering department served the cast freeze-pops during a warm spell. Freeze-pops are a nightmare for the makeup people and continuity because all the actors are liable to end up with orange or yellow tongues after eating them.

(135) The kissing scene with Max and Lucas at the Snow Ball in Stranger Things 2 had to be shot more than once because the camera didn't pick up the reaction of Caleb McLaughlin at first.

(136) Sadie worked with Helen Mirren on her second

Broadway show. This was The Audience.

(137) We see Max watching the short lived television show Misfits of Science in the Stranger Things 4 episode Vecna's Curse. This science fiction comedy series provided an early role for Courteney Cox. It also featured Kevin Peter Hall - a 7 foot tall actor and performer who was later inside the Predator suit in the first two Predator movies.

(138) Sadie is a fan of Emma Watson.

(139) The child extras hired for the Snow Ball scenes were not told at first that they had been hired for Stranger Things 2. They soon worked it out though.

(140) Sadie said that making The Whale gave her much more confidence as an actor and believes this carried over into her performance in Stranger Things 4.

(141) If they hadn't got permission to use Running Up That Hill by Kate Bush in Stranger Things 4, Ross Duffer said that the cover of Dear Prudence by Siouxsie and the Banshees was under consideration as an alternative. Another song under consideration was All We Ever Wanted Is Everything by Bauhaus.

(142) Sadie enjoys looking at TikToks.

(143) The Creel House in Stranger Things 4 is really the Claremont House in Rome, Georgia. This seven bedroom house was built in 1882. Late in 2022, it was reported that the house was up for sale at an asking price of $1.5 million. So, if you have $1.5 million burning a hole in your pocket then a slice of Stranger Things history could be yours.

(144) The Claremont House appealed to the Duffers because it rather evoked The Well House, also known as the Haunted House, in Stephen King's IT.

(145) Sadie supports the New York Pet Rescue charities.

(146) Sadie said the app she uses the most is google maps.

(147) The entry to the afterparty for Stranger Things 2 was fashioned after the Hawkins Town Fair.

(149) At the Stranger Things 2 premiere, the Hawkins Fair themed party served corn dogs, funnel cakes, fresh donuts, and cocktails such as the UpCider Down, the Maple Bourbon Bone Chiller, and Pumpkin Ale.

(150) Sadie was fourteen when she joined the cast of Stranger Things.

(151) Sadie signed to the WME agency in 2022. WME represent famous names like Matt Damon, Jake Gyllenhaal, Conan O'Brien, Joaquin Phoenix, and Hugh Jackman.

(152) Sadie said she was at 'speech and debate practice' when she was telephoned by the Duffers telling her she'd got the part of Max in Stranger Things.

(153) Sadie's parents have a house in New Jersey so she thinks of that house as home - even if she's away a lot.

(154) Sadie said she grew up in a sports mad family but she and her brother Mitchell were different because they were obsessed with musicals and films.

(155) Sadie said she went back to school after appearing on

Broadway because she wanted to feel like a 'normal' person again.

(156) Sadie is a fan of Natalie Portman.

(157) Stranger Things 4 required an incredible 300 days of shooting before it was in the can. The cast must have felt like they had been shooting it forever when they were finally allowed to depart and move onto other things.

(158) Shooting Stranger Things 4 was quite complex because of the pandemic protocols. The cast had to wear masks on the set and be separated during lunch.

(159) Sadie says her favourite book is Of Mice and Men. Of Mice and Men is a novella written by John Steinbeck, first published in 1937.

(160) Sadie says that sudden fame can be quite overwhelming at times.

(161) Stranger Things 3 was viewed by more than 60 million households in its first month. This was a record for a Netflix show.

(162) Sadie is a fan of Reese Witherspoon.

(163) The Madonna song Material Girl plays when Max and Eleven visit Starcourt Mall in Stranger Things 3. Material Girl was the second single from Madonna's Like a Virgin album and released on January 23, 1985.

(164) Sadie said that being cast in Stranger Things was a very big deal because all of her friends watched the show.

(165) Sadie said she took a few tumbles when she did her skateboarding training for Stranger Things 2.

(166) Sadie turned twenty years-old while shooting The Whale.

(167) The Palace Arcade in Stranger Things 2 is named after the 20 Grand Palace Arcade in the 1983 Cold War teen fantasy film WarGames. The arcade was a renovated laundromat located on 6500 Church Street in Douglasville, Georgia. The local people in Douglasville were said to be disappointed when they learned the arcade was not permanent and only for scenes in Stranger Things 2. It was so authentic they thought it was a real arcade someone had opened. The machines in the arcade were real and the Duffers and the crew played on them between takes

(168) Arcade historians thought that the most unrealistic thing about the Palace Arcade was how clean and bright it looked. A busy eighties arcade, with a high turnover of children and teenagers, would almost certainly have been more grubby and arcades didn't tend to waste too much money on decor or lighting. You could explain away the Palace Arcade appearing so pristine and bright by the fact that it seems to be a relatively new business in Hawkins. The building used for the arcade was filthy when the production team found it. The crew had to do a big clean-up job and put a lot of work into making it look like an eighties arcade.

(169) Dacre Montgomery improvised the scene in Will the Wise where Billy grabs Max by the wrist. Dacre Montgomery and Sadie worked on this moment together before the scene was shot so that it would be safe and Sadie would be prepared.

(170) Sadie was a fan of the television show Teen Wolf.

(171) One of Sadie's favourite films is Booksmart.

(172) Roads named Mt. Sinai, Cornwallis, and Kerley in Stranger Things are references to real places in North Carolina where the Duffer Brothers were raised.

(173) Sadie has done endorsement work for Chopard, Prada, Givenchy Beauty, Chanel, Maria Nila, L'OFFICIEL PARIS on her Instagram account.

(174) Sadie said she laughed when she saw Jamie Campbell Bower in his Vecna suit on the Stranger Things 4 set for the first time. I'm not sure this is exactly the reaction they were looking for!

(175) Sadie has attended New York Fashion Week.

(176) The small town of Jackson in Georgia often doubles for (the obviously fictional) Hawkins in Stranger Things. Jackson is nearly fifty miles from the heart of Atlanta and has a population of around 5,000. Those with cafes or stores in Jackson have enjoyed the financial perks of Stranger Things tourists visiting the town. You could probably describe Jackson as a commuter town given its relative proximity to Atlanta. The Town Square of Mulberry Street in Jackson is used the most for shooting in Stranger Things.

(177) Sadie is a fan of Versace.

(178) Sadie is a fan of Bruce Springsteen.

(179) Sadie said that watching Julie Andrews in The Sound of Music inspired her to become an actor and performer.

(180) A Stranger Things novel called Stranger Things:

Runaway Max was written by Brenna Yovanoff. This book sketches a few more details on the life of Max and tells the story of season two from the perspective of this character. There are also flashbacks to her life in California before she arrived in Hawkins. Not that we needed further confirmation after watching Stranger Things 2, but we also learn again in this book that Billy Hargrove is a pain in the you know what. Stranger Things: Runaway Max never quite justifies its existence but if you are a big Stranger Things completist you should find this readable - if never much more than that.

(181) Sadie hasn't done many music videos compared to her Stranger Things co-stars.

(182) The Duffer Brothers say that Stranger Things is not aimed at any age group. It is meant to be enjoyed by everyone. That could be why several networks passed on the show and didn't seem to get the concept. Maybe the networks were puzzled as to whether this was a show for kids or adults. They didn't seem to understand that it was actually BOTH!

(183) Sadie said it was only when she was cast in Stranger Things that she had professional makeup artists. Before this she didn't know much about makeup.

(184) Though Sadie has a Twitter (or X as it is now) account she doesn't seem to be very active on it.

(185) Sadie was speculated to be in line to play Jean Grey in a new X-Men film recently but this turned turned out to be nonsense.

(186) Sadie said she would though consider playing a superhero if an interesting offer came her way.

(187) Max ended Stranger Things 4 in a coma. Sadie said she is completely 'clueless' about whether or not Max will recover. The Duffers keep their plots secret - even from the cast it seems!

(188) Sadie describes herself as a 'selective risk taker' when it comes to acting. She said she wouldn't shy away from a difficult role.

(189) Sadie said she uses a brow gel each day.

(190) There are no reports of Sadie buying her own house yet.

(191) Sadie said she uses fragrance each day now - which is something she didn't do when she was younger.

(192) 361,000 people watched all nine episodes of Stranger Things 2 within the first 24 hours of its release.

(193) Sadie is a huge fan of the film Waiting for Guffman.

(194) Sadie is a fan of Jessica Chastain.

(195) According to The Hawkins Middle School Yearbook/Hawkins High School Yearbook, the ambition of Max Mayfield is to be a professional skateboarder.

(196) Sadie is often seen getting coffee with Stranger Things co-star Gaten Matarazzo because both their families are based in New Jersey.

(197) Sadie says the Max and Eleven mall montage in Stranger Things 3 was great fun to shoot. "There were a lot of revisions for that montage! It was so fun. It took two days to film that montage. It was really great to let loose and not be fighting

back tears or being terrified for once. You need to be silly sometimes."

(198) Polish painter Zdzislaw Beksinski was an influence on the look of the Upside Down in Stranger Things. Beksinski's work was known for its nightmarish dystopian surrealism.

(199) Sadie was the lead in the drama film Dear Zoe in 2022. This film got pretty decent reviews.

(200) Max's terrible feeling in Dear Billy that she can't cheat fate and is probably doomed owes something to the Final Destination horror franchise. In the Final Destination movies the formula has a group of teenagers escaping from some calamitous accident because of premonition but then dying one by one (in enjoyably elaborate and gruesome accidents) because you can't cheat death.

(201) Netflix was founded by by Reed Hastings and Marc Randolph in 1997. They began in the DVD rental market and expanded to streaming in 2010. They entered the content-production industry with House of Cards in 2013.

(202) The younger cast members in Stranger Things started their own group chat they called Stranger Texts. This group chat is apparently defunct now.

(203) Sadie always carries a bottle of water around to stay hydrated.

(204) Streams of 'Running Up that Hill' by Kate Bush increased by an incredible 8,000 percent when Stranger Things 4 was released.

(205) Vecna's hands in Stranger Things 4 contain creepy extra

long clawed fingers. Mechanical metal finger extensions were specially built to add to the Vecna suit by the prosthetics team.

(206) Sadie is a fan of the film Finding Dory.

(207) Sadie loves swimming.

(208) Sadie said she has a strange obsession with HGTV. HGTV (an initialism for Home & Garden Television) is an American pay television channel owned by Warner Bros. Discovery. The network primarily broadcasts reality programming related to home improvement and real estate.

(209) You can now buy Stranger Things action figures, Stranger Things toy cars, and Stranger Things Monopoly.

(210) When we see Bob and Joyce kissing in the store in Stranger Things 2 you can see an Annie wig. This is a probable reference to the fact that Sadie played Annie on the stage.

(211) The name Sadie is Hebrew in origin.

(212) The io9 website wrote of Stranger Things 2 - 'If you liked season one, and pretty much everyone did, then you'll like this season just fine. Everything is turned up a bit, but the soul of Stranger Things remains what it was last season—a story about friendship, family, and giant piles of '80s nostalgia. Stranger Things had an almost impossible task when it came to following up on a first season that had near-universal acclaim. That it's still engaging, gorgeous looking, and smartly written is a truly impressive feat. The show didn't hit any reset buttons; it let every character grow and change, and it's just remarkable. This is a show growing naturally into itself and does everything to make the nine-hour

commitment worth it.'

(213) Sadie is a fan of Amy Adams.

(214) When Steve and the kids take refuge in the bus in the junkyard in Stranger Things 2 this might be another reference to the Mad Max film series - where vehicles are fortified to survive in a post apocalyptic future. MADMAX is the username of Max in the arcade.

(215) Sadie said she isn't 'girly' but not a tomboy. She thinks she sits somewhere in the middle.

(216) Sadie said she sometimes divulges Stranger Things spoilers to her family. She is confident nothing will leak from the Sink household!

(217) Sadie was deemed too tall at first for the part of Max in Stranger Things but the other children had sufficient growth spurts to make sure she wouldn't tower over them.

(218) In addition to her acting skills, Sadie is also a talented singer.

(219) The montage of Eleven and Max shopping at the mall in Stranger Things 3 seems inspired by a similar montage in the cult 1984 film Night of the Comet.

(220) Sadie has a cat named Rocky.

(221) Sadie says she has suffered from anxiety.

(222) Sadie has supported homeless charities.

(223) Sadie has a secret TikTok account.

(224) Sadie thinks that spending too much time on social media can be a bit damaging because the time would be better spent with real people rather than online 'friends'.

(225) Sadie said that when she was a kid all she ever wanted was to appear in a show on Broadway.

(226) Despite her aversion to most horror films, Sadie said she did like Midsommar.

(227) Sadie said that unless she's working she doesn't like leaving the house.

(228) Sadie is a big fan of the television show Grey's Anatomy.

(229) Sadie says that it was Millie Bobby Brown who persuaded the Duffers to make Eleven and Max friends in season three. "Millie definitely made it known to the Duffers that she wanted our characters to be friends. I did, too, but she was much more vocal about it. That was exactly what she wanted."

(230) Sadie said she started writing a journal during the quarantine lockdowns.

(231) Sadie is a fan of the film Mamma Mia!

(232) Sadie said that even when she became famous through Stranger things she was never allowed to get too big for her boots at home and still had to do chores.

(233) Sadie said she thinks Stranger Things is slightly scarier than Fear Street.

(234) Sadie was told to watch some classic slasher movies in

preparation for Fear Street.

(235) Sadie is a big fan of the classic book The Great Gatsby.

The Great Gatsby is a 1925 novel by F Scott Fitzgerald that I'd imagine most people must have read by now. It's a short novel but generally regarded to be one of the greatest works of fiction of the last century. The story is set during the early part of the Roaring Twenties, the Jazz Age. A time of great prosperity for America. Wild parties, prohibition, bootleggers, new money, people becoming rich. It isn't destined to last though. The great stock market crash of 1929 is just around the corner and will serve as the sober hangover and symbolic ending for this glitter strewn decade of excess. The shadows are already beginning to loom well before in the story. It's an era that can't possibly last forever. So the novel is a snapshot of the age among a particular money washed strata of American society before it all goes belly up.

The story is narrated by Nick Carraway, a young man who has moved to Long Island's West Egg from the Midwest to start a new life and work in the New York bond business. Across the bay at East Egg are some old friends he soon becomes reacquainted with and both will play a pivotal part in the story. A couple named Tom and Daisy Buchanan. Nick went to Yale with Tom while Daisy is his second cousin. We soon see for ourselves how bored and superficial Tom and Daisy are despite their wealth and glamour. The less fashionable West Egg is where those with new money live and Nick finds his modest house situated next to the grand mansion of the mysterious and enigmatic Gatsby. Gatsby throws huge swanky champagne sozzled parties at his mansion for the fashionable and rich but he's never actually seen at any of them enjoying himself or taking part in the revelry. Who is Gatsby and to what end does he arrange these lavish parties if he seems to have little interest in them and largely keeps himself to himself?

(236) Sadie was nominated for the Critics' Choice Movie Award for Best Young Performer for her performance in The Whale.

(237) The film that Steve sneaks Max and the kids in to watch at the mall at the start of Stranger Things 3 is George A Romero's Day of the Dead - an enjoyably gruesome and cultish zombie film. The film was unrated so the kids would definitely not have been allowed in by conventional means. Day of the Dead is the last part of Romero's classic zombie trilogy and follows on from Night of the Living Dead and Dawn of the Dead. Dawn of the Dead was set in a shopping mall so this film was definitely an influence on Stranger Things 3.

(238) In 2019, 13% of former Netflix subscribers rejoined the streaming platform specifically to watch Stranger Things 3. Stranger Things has obviously been a big moneymaker for Netflix and is probably the most important show they've ever had in terms of revenue.

(239) The make-up department on Stranger Things have sometimes used coffee granules to depict the muddied faces of those who have been exposed to the Upside Down.

(240) Sadie said that when she first heard that Taylor Swift was trying to contact her she thought it was a hoax! Sadie thought it was scammers trying to get hold of her details. Thankfully though it really was Taylor Swift.

(241) Stranger Things didn't get a single nomination at the Golden Globes at the end of 2022. Most fans of the show found this rather bizarre. A lot of people, including Stranger Things

producer and director Shawn Levy, thought that Sadie deserved an Emmy nomination for her work in Stranger Things 4.

(242) It seems that literally everyone in the Stranger Things cast wants to be a singer. Finn Wolfhard, Joe Keery, Maya Hawke, and Gaten Materazzo have all been in bands or music in conjunction with the show and while she hasn't taken the plunge yet there is always speculation, whether accurate or inaccurate, that Sadie might have a bash at a singing career one day. It seems more plausible to think that Sadie might sing on the stage again one day rather than launch a solo singing career.

(243) Sadie says it was slightly strange to act out scenes in Stranger Things 2 where she hates Billy because in real life she and Dacre Montgomery (who played Billy) are good friends. Dacre is obviously nothing like Billy in real life.

(244) Max uses the word 'zoomer' in Stranger Thing 2. This is a modern term for Generation X. It is not an anachronism in Stranger Things though because Max is presumably making reference to liking fast things

(245) The Fear Street films are based on books by R.L. Stine - who has been dubbed the Stephen King of children's literature. Stine has written gazillions of books.

(246) Sadie had never actually read any R.L. Stine books before she was cast in Fear Street.

(247) Sadie is an Aries.

(248) Sadie said she keeps in touch with the Stranger Things cast through FaceTime. They don't see each too much away

from the show because work and family life means they are often scattered around in different places.

(249) The Duffers said they actually considered killing Max off in Stranger Things 4 - though they obviously didn't do this in the end. One imagines Sadie would have been a bit annoyed if they'd done this because she would have missed out on Stranger Things 5!

(250) You can now buy a Sadie Sink customised coffee mug. This is 'unofficial' merch. Sadie doesn't have a slice of this sort of stuff and is probably oblivious to its existence.

(251) Sadie often wears a cap in public in order to be more incognito. A lot of celebrities do this because it must be a bit annoying to have to sign autographs when you've just popped out to get a cup of coffee or something.

(252) The stylist Molly Dickson chooses the outfits Sadie. Molly Dickson has also worked as a stylist for big stars like Scarlett Johansson.

(253) Sadie wore a Miu Miu dress at the 2018 Golden Globes.

(254) A demographic breakdown of Stranger Things viewers showed it was very popular with females as women and girls accounted for 57% of the audience.

(255) Sadie said she would describe herself as a feminist.

(256) Sadie was used to promote Givenchy Beauty's Le Rouge Deep Velvet lipstick.

(257) Winona Ryder, who plays Joyce Byers in Stranger Things, said of Sadie - "Sadie is like Liv Ullmann. She's going

to be like Meryl Streep."

(258) Sadie said when she uses a fragrance that two sprays is her limit. Sadie thinks that less is more when it comes to fragrance.

(259) Sadie said that when she was cast in Stranger Things 2, apart from some bronzer, her hair and clothes as Max were more or less the same as how she looked in real life!

(260) Sadie doesn't believe that fame has changed her as a person. She thinks she is still very down to earth and normal away from the camera.

(261) Sadie said that she lives in her own little 'bubble' and doesn't have a 'celebrity' sort of life.

(262) Sadie said that if she could live in any fictional universe it would be the Disney universe.

(263) Sadie said she often goes to bed at 9:30 pm! She's definitely not a night person then.

(264) Sadie is a fan of the television show Euphoria. The series stars Zendaya as Rue Bennett. Euphoria has been praised for its realistic portrayal of teenage life and its bold storytelling.

(265) Netflix apparently wanted to shoot seasons two and three of Stranger Things back to back so the children would not appear to visibly age but the Duffers vetoed this plan as they felt that it would put too much strain on the writing and production of the show. The Duffers also felt that the young cast members visibly changing from season to season was not necessarily a bad thing and made the show more interesting.

(266) Sadie said that a salient reason (besides loving animals obviously) why she became a vegan is that she had a three day sleepover with Woody Harrelson's daughter where they ate nothing but vegan food. Sadie said the vegan food was great and so realised it would be no great hardship to eat this sort of food all the time.

(267) Sadie had to do a table read as an audition for her part in The Whale. This was quite nerve-wracking but unavoidable. They don't tend to give actors a part in a film unless they do a good audition!

(268) Sadie said she was very nervous the first time she watched The Whale in the cinema with an audience. This was a special screening at a film festival.

(269) Sadie attended the Le Grand Numero De Chanel Fragance Show at Le Grand Palais Ephemere in 2022.

(270) Sadie said her friends sometimes call her 'grandma' because she's a bit old-fashioned and likes the quiet life. Sadie isn't a crazy party animal sort of celebrity.

(271) While he was in the makeup chair being transformed into the monstrous villain Vecna on the set of Stranger Things 4, Jamie Campbell Bower would play some thrash metal tunes to help him get into character. Ironically, another song he listened to a lot was Placebo's cover of Running Up That Hill.

(272) Sadie has appeared as a guest on The Kelly Clarkson Show.

(273) The episode of Blue Bloods that Sadie appeared in was called Insult to Injury. Blue Bloods is a police show set in New York that stars (among others) Tom Selleck and Donnie

Wahlberg. The show is about a family who have a long tradition of serving as police officers.

(274) Sadie was a presenter at the American Music Awards in 2017.

(275) A survey once found 31% of young adults had watched all the episodes of Stranger Things. Another 17% of respondents said they had seen at least some of the show and intended to watch more in the future.

(276) Most of the networks who rejected Stranger Things wanted the show to lose the kids and just focus on Hopper as the central character. These networks made a big mistake because not only was Stranger Things hugely popular it was the kids in the show who went a long way to making it so successful.

(277) Sadie attended the Nickelodeon Kids' Choice Awards in 2018.

(278) Sadie has appeared as a guest on Good Morning America. As the name suggests, this is a breakfast television show.

(279) Sadie has appeared on Late Night with Seth Myers.

(280) Sadie has appeared on Días de cine. This is a Spanish show about cinema.

(281) Joe Keery (who plays Steve Harrington) nearly hit Sadie with Steve's nail spiked baseball bat shooting Stranger Things 2. Naturally, the bat is a prop so no great harm would have been caused. The sequence where Sadie nearly got a wallop from the prop bat was at the mist shrouded junkyard where the DemoDogs sneak up on Steve and the kids.

(282) Brenham, where Sadie was born, is most famous for being the home of Blue Bell Creameries. Blue Bell is one of the biggest selling ice-cream brands in the United States.

(283) Sadie will doubtless be pleased to know that Blue Bell are now offering some vegan versions of their ice-cream.

(284) In their review of Sadie's stage role as Annie, The Houston Chronicle wrote - "The sun comes out every time Sink's Annie marches on stage. She's a natural - feisty but not overbearing, wistful yet tough and resilient, and she sings with the force, confidence and conviction of a pro."

(285) Sadie said, when she's alone, she often sings and whistles songs from Annie purely for fun. She must know them all by heart after Broadway.

(286) Sadie studied at TUTS' Humphreys School of Musical Theatre. This is based in Houston.

(287) Sadie also studied at Houston Family Arts Center's summer camp.

(288) Sadie said that as a kid she would sing and perform plays with her brother Mitchell at home. Sadie said her other two brothers were more into American football.

(289) At the eight of eight, Sadie played Mary in a stage production of The Secret Garden.

(290) The Palace Arcade in Stranger Things 2 has the following games - Dragon's Lair, Dig-Dug, Asteroids, Galaga, Centipede and Pac-Man. You also see a game called Quest for the Space Knife but this is a fictitious game and a joke reference to one of the production crew of Stranger Things

having a music group called Space Knife. If you look fast you'll also see a poster for a movie called Quest for the Space Knife in the cinema lobby in season two.

(291) Hasbro have released a Stranger Things Palace Arcade Handheld Electronic Game. The device allows you to play twenty vintage games which include Pac-Man, Dig Dug, Galaga, and Galaxian.

(292) Darren Aronofsky, who directed The Whale, said of Sadie - "Sadie is as precise as a surgeon's scalpel. She's a firecracker of emotion and a complete professional."

(293) At the end of Stranger Things 2, one theory floated by some fans was the suggestion that Billy and Max's family are Soviet spies who have been embedded in the United States. While this theory did not turn out to be true they were least right about the Soviets turning up in Hawkins!

(294) Sadie thinks that the stage is the best place to start acting because it teaches you a lot of important disciplines like punctuality, how to work in a big cast, and how to project a performance.

(295) Sadie was cast in a HBO series called Utopia in 2015 which was going to be made by David Fincher. However, the project collapsed when Fincher and HBO could not agree on the budget. If the show had gone ahead then Sadie would not have been available to audition for Stranger Things 2. In hindsight, the cancellation of Utopia was a blessing in disguise for Sadie's career because she would have missed out on Stranger Things. Utopia later went ahead in 2020 with a different cast and no David Fincher but was scrapped after eight episodes.

(296) Sadie, like most kids in the entertainment industry it seems, was homeschooled when she worked on the stage but later went to a real school.

(297) Sadie is a big fan of the musical Matilda.

(298) Sadie is a big fan of the musical comedy You're a Good Man, Charlie Brown.

(299) Sadie is a fan of the pop rock band The 1975.

(300) Sadie said it is difficult sometimes to balance fame and acting with a normal life away from the camera.

(301) Sadie shot a film called Berlin Nobody in 2022. As the title implies, Sadie had to go to Berlin to make this film.

(302) Sadie said that when she gets recognised in public it is always the red hair that always gives her away.

(303) Sadie said that red carpet events still feel a bit weird to do. They are obviously unavoidable though if you are an actor.

(304) Sadie said she would never dye her hair.

(305) The premiere of Stranger Things 2 was Sadie's first ever red carpet event.

(306) If one were to compile a top table of the greatest ever Stranger Things episodes then Dear Billy would have a strong case for inclusion. This is the episode where Stranger Things 4 accelerates into top gear - culminating in a truly amazing third act. Dear Billy is surely Sadie's finest hour in the show.

(307) The 'happy place' that Max travels to in her mind to escape from Vecna in Stranger Things 4 is the Snow Ball dance from the season two finale. However, this proves to be unsuccessful and she is found. This is explained by the fact that at the end of season two we saw that the Flayer - an extension of Vecna - was ominously watching over (or under if you prefer) Hawkins as the Snow Ball took place.

(308) When Sadie did her skateboarding training for Stranger Things 2, her co-star Finn Wolfhard joined in sometimes to help out as he is a pretty nifty skateboarder in real life.

(309) Sadie said she got teased for having red hair at school but loves it now because its her 'signature'.

(310) A lot of the younger cast members in Stranger Things besides have a stage background. Gaten Matarazzo, Caleb McLaughlin, and Gabriella Pizzolo (who plays Suzie), had all appeared on Broadway prior to being cast in Stranger Things.

(311) When they began shooting Stranger Things 2, the crew noticed drones in the sky above the set attempting to capture footage. This was a far cry from season one - which was filmed in relative obscurity.

(312) Sadie said that having shorter hair is much nicer in hot weather than long hair.

(313) The house of Heather the lifeguard in Stranger Things 3, which Max and Eleven have to visit, is deliberately similar to Heather Langenkamp's house in Wes Craven's A Nightmare on Elm Street.

(314) Sadie is a fan of the actress Julianne Moore.

(315) Stranger Things 2 had a budget of $8 million per episode. This was fairly generous but the budget would soon get much higher.

(316) Sadie says she doesn't wear eyeliner or mascara in real life - only for photoshoots and events.

(317) Most of the Starcourt Mall scenes in Stranger Things 3 made use of Gwinnett Place Mall's huge atrium space. The mall was perfect for the needs of the production because it had plenty of room for cameras and even a large balcony.

(318) Sadie said that Kate Winslet in Titanic is a big beauty icon to her because Kate has red hair in that film.

(319) Dart was depicted by a rubber toy on the set of Stranger Things 2. The digital effects for Dart were added in post-production.

(320) The Starcourt Mall in Stranger Things 3 set had an operational food court and real hot food was constantly prepared for background extras to eat in scenes.

(321) The Duffer Brothers said that casting the right children in Stranger Things was the most important task they had. A gratingly bad performance from just one of the child actors could potentially have sunk the whole show.

(322) Sadie was seen wearing denim overalls in New York in 2023.

(323) Sadie is a fan of Lily James.

(324) The Duffer Brothers think they should have used the Palace Arcade more in Stranger Things 2. They don't think

they came up with enough arcade scenes.

(325) Sadie is a big fan of Tilda Swinton.

(326) Although things are not perfect and there is still some way to go, Sadie thinks there are more opportunities for women in the film industry than there used to be.

(327) Despite being in Stranger Things, Sadie said she prefers 90s makeup and fashion to 80s makeup and fashion.

(328) Sadie said that after The Whale and Stranger Things 4 she is now starting to be sent really 'exciting' scripts to read. Her star is on the rise.

(329) Sadie said she 'leaned' on Millie Bobby Brown a lot while making Stranger Things 2 because Millie was the only other girl in the cast.

(330) After making The Whale, Brendan Fraser said of Sadie - "Her talent precedes her years of experience. I watched her every day just get the gold star in every way that I have not seen a young actor know how to be that precise, that inventive; how to be that consistent; to have that perfect elocution without being affected."

(331) Sadie said her brothers are big fans of Stranger Things. It was exciting for them when their sister got a plum role in the show.

(332) Sadie's favourite song is Upside Down by Jack Johnson. That title is very appropriate for a Stranger Things star!

(333) When Sadie joined the cast of Stranger Things, Winona Ryder recognised Sadie from The Americans because that is

Winona's favourite show!

(334) Sadie and Maya Hawke were on hand to support Stranger Things co-star Gaten Matarazzo when he made his debut in the stage show Dear Evan Hansen in 2022.

(335) Stranger Things is shot on a digital cinema camera but to achieve the vintage look a layer of scanned film grain was added to the colouring process.

(336) EUE/Screen Gems Studios, where Stranger Things is made, is a 10-stage, 33-acre Atlanta studio complex.

(337) Sadie has one of her finest acting moments in Dear Billy where Max laments the fact that she always felt luckless and cursed - even before Vecna came along. Almost in gallows humour, Max declares that it came as no surprise then to learn that Vecna was now on her case.

(338) An episode of Stranger Things will usually take about two weeks to shoot. The special effects are another matter entirely though. They take a lot longer than two weeks to complete. In a sense shooting the stuff with the actors is the easiest part of the show from a production point of view. The digital effects though are increasingly complex and time consuming to complete.

(339) Sadie said she suffered a bit from 'impostor syndrome' when she became famous. This was basically self-doubt.

(340) Urethane resins, rope, pool noodles and bubble wrap were used to create the icky vines of the Upside Down in Stranger Things.

(341) Sadie said when she hit the catwalk as a model they gave

her huge heels because she isn't the tallest person in the world.

(342) Though time is usually in short supply on a production as big as a season of Stranger Things, the Duffers will usually allow the actors to rehearse a scene a few hours before it is actually shot.

(343) As you might expect of a Broadway kid, Sadie likes a bit of karaoke now and again.

(344) There seems to be a Jeffrey Dahmer Easter egg in Stranger Things 4 when Max gets off the bus and a kid who looks the dead spit of Dahmer (right down to the aviator spectacles) walks past in the background. The miniseries Monster: The Jeffrey Dahmer Story dropped on Netflix in fairly close proximity to Stranger Things 4 so this doesn't seem like a coincidence. The Duffers have not officially acknowledged if the kid REALLY was supposed to a Dahmer reference though. Jeffrey Dahmer was an infamous serial killer.

(345) Sadie seems to be fond of fruit smoothies. She is often seen clutching a smoothie drink when 'papped' by photographers in the street.

(346) Stranger Things 4 was the most watched Netflix show in 92 countries. Such is the global appeal of the show that some industry commentators wonder how on earth Netflix will cope when this pop culture juggernaut comes to an end. How can they possibly replace Stranger Things?

(347) Sadie has an AC/DC t-shirt. AC/DC are a heavy metal band.

(348) Stranger Things 4 accrued 7.2 billion minutes of streaming viewership in the United States from May 30 to June 5 in 2022.

(349) Sadie has featured in Teen Vogue.

(350) Stranger Things 4 was the first season of the show to be released in two parts. Previous seasons were dropped on Netflix in their entirety and rabidly binged in short order from start to finish by fans. It was widely assumed at the time that some cynical Netflix number crunching was responsible for the season being split into two parts. The theory was that Netflix wanted to stop people unsubscribing after watching Stranger Things 4 - so they split it up. You'd now have to keep Netflix in order to watch the rest of the season (or two episodes to be precise) at a later date. It turned out though that this presumption wasn't actually correct. The reason why we had to wait for the last batch of episodes is that the special effects were still being tweaked.

(351) When she was a little kid, Sadie was in a commercial for Pixma cannon printers.

(352) You can now buy, should you ever desire one, a Sadie Sink cardboard face mask.

(353) Vecna follows in the tradition of Stranger Things villains in that it is inspired by Dungeons & Dragons but not strictly the same thing as its board game counterpart. A big influence on Vecna in Stranger Things was the Night King in Game of Thrones.

(354) Sadie seems to be fond of wrist bracelets.

(355) The Netflix streaming service overloaded and crashed

for about half an hour when Volume 2 of Stranger Things 4 was dropped on the site.

(356) Sadie said it took a season or two before she stopped feeling like the 'new kid' in Stranger Things.

(357) There is no clear official consensus on the best or worst season of Stranger Things because these things are naturally subjective. The critic ratings on Rotten Tomatoes rank the seasons in order with season one the highest rated and season four the lowest. This would appear to be a contradiction to the general view that Stranger Things 4 was a return to form and an improvement over season three. The audience ratings on RT are more or less the same pattern as the critic ratings - though with seasons three and four tied for last. Stranger Things 4 could possibly be a victim of the fact there are simply more reviews - which make it more vulnerable to the sniffy critic determined to nitpick the show and be a party pooper. IMDB, by contrast, has higher ratings for the season four episodes as a whole than the season three ones - which feels about right.

(358) Sadie is considered to be alarmingly normal for a celebrity. She is never in gossip columns and lives a quiet ordinary life away from the camera.

(359) Sadie has modelled for Kate Spade.

(360) The average length of a Stranger Things episode is 61 minutes. This is mostly due to season four - which had an average episode length of 86 minutes. That was considerably longer than than the previous three seasons. There is no standard length for an episode of the show. They can run for however long the Duffer Brothers decide.

(361) Sadie said that when she was shooting The Whale the heating in her accommodation conked out so she was freezing cold!

(362) The cast of Fear Street 2 were given a list of songs to listen to in order to get them into a 1970s mood.

(363) The surname Sink is of English and German origin.

(364) Sadie wore dangle earrings with pink quartz and rubellites to the Golden Globes in 2018.

(365) Sadie has done a photoshoot for Schön! Magazine.

(366) Annie tells the story of a young orphan named Annie who lives in a New York City orphanage run by the mean Miss Hannigan. Annie's luck changes when she is chosen to spend Christmas at the mansion of billionaire Oliver Warbucks. As Annie charms everyone she meets, including Warbucks, she begins to melt his heart and learns about the true meaning of family. The musical features beloved songs such as Tomorrow, It's the Hard Knock Life, and Maybe.

(367) The Duffer Brothers say that one of the reasons why they relate to Stranger Things and created it in the first place is that they were born in 1984 and so were the last generation of kids who grew up remembering what life was like before the internet and everyone (and I mean EVERYONE) walking around glued to their mobile telephones. The Duffer Brothers had memories of the pre-digital age and liked the idea of a show set in those times.

(368) The Fear Street books are known for their interconnected stories and recurring characters, often spanning multiple books.

(369) Although it was quite a prestigious project, The Whale got decidedly mixed reviews. It stands at 64% on Rotten Tomatoes.

(370) Jamie Campbell Bower needed 25 pieces of latex and silicone rubber glued to his body to transform into Vecna. The reason they wanted an actor in a suit for Vecna is that they wanted to go back to the DNA of season one where the Demogorgon was mostly Mark Steger in an elaborate monster suit. The fact that Bower was on the set as Vecna interacting with the actors was a great advantage because if Vecna had been a special effect then the cast would have had to react to a tennis ball on a piece of string or something and Vecna would have been added in months later as a digital effect.

(371) The costume department on Stranger Things 3 had fun planning the mall montage with Eleven and Max. If you look carefully during Stranger Things 3 you will see extras at the mall dressed as Hulk Hogan, Boy George, and Madonna.

(372) Sadie said she found the Milkman killer the scariest character in Fear Street.

(373) What makes the final sequence in Dear Billy of Max trying to escape from Vecna all the more moving is that Max is essentially trying to outrun depression and unhappiness. She is running back to the person she used to be.

(374) Unlike R. L Stine's other popular series, Goosebumps, Fear Street caters to a slightly older audience, delving into darker themes and more mature content.

(375) Sadie's brother Mitchell appeared in the show Elf on Broadway.

(376) Sadie said her wardrobe at home is a bit cluttered with designer clothes she was given or wore on the red carpet but has no reason to wear again.

(377) Sadie said she enjoys watching old movies.

(378) Sadie is a vocal advocate for sustainability and protecting the environment.

(379) Sadie said that when you work in the entertainment industry as a kid you tend to mature quicker than you might otherwise have done because you are surrounded by adults all the time.

(380) The Whale was filmed in Newburgh, New York.

(381) Sadie said in 2023 that the Duffer Brothers can't get their heads around the fact that some of the Stranger Things 'kids' are now in their twenties. Time has flown past.

(382) Sadie attended the Governors Awards in 2022. The Governors Awards presentation is an annual award ceremony hosted by the Academy of Motion Picture Arts and Sciences (AMPAS).

(383) Sadie wore a Prada Custom Jumpsuit at the Stranger Things 3 premiere.

(384) Sadie has attended some comic cons to promote Stranger Things - not that it needs much promoting.

(385) For the screening of All Too Well: A Short Film at the Toronto Film Festival, Sade wore a Stella McCartney blazer and trousers.

(386) Stephen King is a big fan of Stranger Things. He called it 'Steve King's greatest hits' (King was obviously referencing the fact that Stranger Things riffs on a number of his books).

(387) The Duffers sometimes play spooky music on the set of Stranger Things to get the actors in the right mood to convey fear and tension for scary scenes. During the mist blanketed junkyard sequence in Stranger Things 2 the crew played the Close Encounters soundtrack.

(388) Sadie owns some Alexander McQueen boots.

(389) Sadie said she learned a lot from Helen Mirren when they appeared on Broadway together in The Audience.

(390) Believe it or not, James Corden was set to play the lead part in The Whale before Brendan Fraser came onboard. This was under a different director named Tom Ford. Ford and Corden left the project in the end though.

(391) Sadie thinks the character of Max Mayfield in Stranger Things is more sarcastic and emotionally distant than she is in real life.

(392) Sadie was the cover star for the magazine Fashion in September 2022.

(393) Sadie said - "My happy resolution is to explore new hobbies and interests that are going to bring me joy beyond my work. And to make sure that I'm surrounding myself with people who uplift me and motivate me to be my best and happiest self."

(394) Sadie likes to play board games with her family.

(395) In 2021, Sadie became the face of Chopard's Happy Diamonds.

(396) Sadie must have felt at home making Fear Street 2 because, like Stranger Things, it was made in Georgia and Maya Hawke (who plays Robin in Stranger Things) was part of the cast.

(397) Sadie and co-star Dylan O'Brien improvised some of the scenes in the Taylor Swift film All Too Well.

(398) Sadie was described as a "burgeoning scream queen" by the AV Club in their review of Stranger Things 4.

(399) One of the people who does the subtitles for Stranger Things said that using the words 'tentacles undulating moistly' to describe the sound effects of Vecna in his lair was done as a bit of a joke.

(400) Some fans think that Stranger Things 2 missed a trick by not having Polybius in the Palace Arcade. Polybius is a fictitious arcade game and the subject of an urban myth. The urban legend describes the game as part of a government-run psychology experiment based in Portland, Oregon, during 1981. Gameplay supposedly produced intense psychoactive and addictive effects in the player. These few publicly staged arcade machines were said to have been visited periodically by men in black for the purpose of data-mining the machines and analyzing these effects. Eventually, all of these Polybius arcade machines allegedly disappeared from the arcade market.

(401) The play The Audience is about Queen Elizabeth II and her secret talks with various prime ministers.

(402) Sadie said that appearing in The Audience gave her a crash course in British political history.

(403) Sadie is a big fan of the film Back to the Future.

(404) The fame of Stranger Things is such that it was the subject of an affectionate Sesame Street parody in 2017. It features Cookie Monster as the Cookiegorgon!

(405) There is no official confirmation that Sadie has any tattoos yet. It is quite rare for a young celebrity not to have a tattoo!

(406) Although she was born in Texas, Sadie has spent half of her life around New York.

(407) Sadie said she didn't have much confidence when she was at school but feels bolder now.

(408) The Shadow Monster in Stranger Things 2 was largely inspired by volcanic eruptions and lightning storms.

(409) Sadie said she once swiped a 'warming' hoodie jacket from the Stranger Things costume department and took it home. Sadie said it was an honest mistake!

(410) Atlanta was chosen as the shooting location for Stranger Things because the production team found that the surrounding areas had a very 'anytown' feel. With some modifications they could made to look very generic Americana.

(411) Sadie is a fan of vegan cinnamon rolls. Cinnamon rolls are a delicious and sweet pastry made with a soft and fluffy dough, cinnamon filling, and topped with icing or glaze.

(412) Sadie is a fan of raspberries.

(413) Sadie said that when you work as a child actor on Broadway you always end up knowing all the kids from the other shows.

(414) Sadie was allowed to keep and take home the green VANS trainers (sneakers) that Max wore in Stranger Things 2. Sadie they are a bit worn and battered but make a nice memento from her time on the show.

(415) Sadie says she is a bit superstitious. She said, for example, that when she went to her Stranger Things auditions she always sat in the same spot in the car because she had come to believe it was somehow good luck.

(416) Sadie said her mother filmed her reaction to getting the part of Max in Stranger Things. Sadie says she looks completely astonished and stunned in the video!

(417) Sadie said a standard outfit for her would be jeans and a blazer.

(418) Sadie says she has some towering platform trainers that she can't really wear anywhere because they aren't exactly casual footwear for going down the shop!

(419) Sadie is partial to some french fries. Who isn't?

(420) The smoke monster in Stranger Things 2 looks like it might have been inspired by Maman by the artist Louise Bourgeois. Mamam is a bronze and marble sculpture that looks like a giant spider.

(421) A Max Mayfield Funko Pop signed by Sadie can fetch up

to £400 online.

(422) Sadie said she enjoys some of the Stranger Things art that fans post online.

(423) Sadie said it is a bit frightening to think of how many people in the world watch Stranger Things. The show has millions of viewers in many different countries.

(424) Sadie is a fan of the television show Ozark. Ozark is a popular American crime drama television series created by Bill Dubuque. The show first premiered in 2017 and is available to stream on Netflix. It follows the story of a financial planner, Marty Byrde, who is forced to relocate his family from Chicago to the Ozarks after a money-laundering scheme goes wrong.

(425) Sadie is a fan of the miniseries Inventing Anna. The show follows the rise and fall of Anna Sorokin, a Russian-born con artist who posed as a wealthy German heiress and scammed her way into New York City's elite social scene.

(426) Sadie said it was quite strange doing the press junkets for The Whale because she is used to having the Stranger Things kids with her on press tours.

(427) When the film version of Stephen King's It with (Sadie's Stranger Things co-star) Finn Wolfhard came out, Sadie was asked if she'd seen it but said she was scared to watch it. That was several years ago now so maybe she's watched it since then?

(428) David Harbour said that shooting Stranger Things 2 was a good decompression chamber for the kids in the show because they were insulated from fame and were allowed to

relax, goof around on the set and just be kids.

(429) When she was cast in Stranger Things 2, Sadie said she was dreading her social media notifications going crazy once the show aired.

(430) Sadie and the cast called Finn Wolfhard 'Emo Mike' shooting Stranger Things 2 because Mike is quite sulky and depressed in season two at the loss of Eleven.

(431) Sadie describes her life away from the camera as quite 'boring' but says she wouldn't have it any other way.

(432) Buzzfeed named Sadie as Max in Stranger Things 4 the fourth best television acting performance of 2022.

(433) According to a poll by the survey site YouGov, 45% of people in America have heard of Sadie Sink.

(434) Millie Bobby Brown is the only Stranger Things cast member with more Instagram followers than Sadie.

(435) American Odyssey, which Sadie was in, was an action thriller series on NBC. It was cancelled after one season in 2015.

(436) Sadie says that her brother Mitchell is her best friend.

(437) Sadie said she quite likes the idea of being the lead in an action film one day.

(438) Sadie graduated from high school.

(439) Sadie said she had to work on her fitness and stamina for Fear Street because the part required a lot of running.

(440) Sadie said that after doing Stranger Things and Fear Street she is pretty good at screaming on cue for the camera!

(441) Sadie said it was a great relief to go back to work after the pandemic.

(442) Sadie said the worst thing you can do in the acting industry is feel like you are in competition with other actors.

(443) Sadie finds the colour blue calming.

(444) Sadie expressed her support for the Black Lives Matter movement in 2020.

(445) Sadie has been involved with The Gentle Barn, a sanctuary for rescued animals.

(446) In 2018, Sadie, at 15, became the youngest participant to take to the catwalk at Paris Fashion Week.

(447) In the 2017 Stranger Things computer game, Max Mayfield has psychic powers. This is definitely not canon with the show!

(448) The shooting location for Forest Hills trailer park in Stranger Things 4 where Max Mayfield lives was Griffin, Georgia.

(449) Stranger Things 2 costume designer Kim Wilcox says she scoured Tiger Beat and Cosmopolitan magazines, as well as old Sears and J.C. Penney's catalogues for inspiration when it came to dressing Sadie and the other young characters.

(450) Sadie said that even as a little kid she did research on any role she had to play.

(451) Sadie said she never reads Stranger Things fan theories. She probably has no need to because she's in the show!

(452) Netflix had to draft special effects experts from their other shows in order to complete the complex special effects on Stranger Things 4. If they hadn't done that we'd probably still be waiting for season four to be released today!

(453) Sadie thinks that, out the Stranger Things cast, David Harbour would have the best chance of surviving in the Upside Down because he's very smart.

(454) Sadie said the school she went to in New Jersey was a bit 'preppy' - the sort of place where brands and clothes are status symbols.

(455) Sadie says that Noah Schnapp is the Stranger Things cast member most likely to steal something from the set!

(456) You can see a Time-Out arcade in the mall in Stranger Things 3. Time-Out Amusement Centers were a chain of arcades located in malls across America. The first one opened in 1970.

(457) Sadie likes dairy free peanut butter ice cream.

(458) Believe it or not, you can now buy kitchen sponges made to look like Stranger Things VHS tapes.

(459) Sadie has promoted campaigns to reduce plastic waste.

(460) The Duffers said that Stranger Things 4 was inspired (among a great many other things) by The Empire Strikes Back in that the characters almost seem to lose in the end.

(461) Sadie seems to be very fond of sunglasses.

(462) There is a copy of Mad Max in the Family Video store in Stranger Things 3. Mad Max is a 1979 Australian dystopian action thriller film directed by George Miller and featured a young Mel Gibson. This film inspired the title of the opening episode of season two - MADMAX.

(463) Sadie said that her Stranger Things co-star Maya Hawke is a big inspiration to her.

(464) Sadie thinks that her character Ziggy in Fear Street is a bit more mature than Max Mayfield in Stranger Things.

(465) Sadie said that it is nice to clear your schedule and take a break from acting and media work when you have the chance.

(466) The popularity of video game arcades like the one in Stranger Things 2 began to dwindle in the 1990s. The obvious factor in this was that the video games you could play at home were rapidly getting better and better and giving you an arcade experience from the comfort of your bedroom (where you also didn't need to have a bag of coins in order to play). If you could play games like Doom and Quake at home why would you need to go to an arcade anymore? Shopping malls eventually began to sell their arcade machines because they were no longer profitable and the demise of the video game arcade began. As a reaction to the revolution and quantum leap in home gaming, arcades introduced motion simulator arcade machines like Typhoon where you would be thrown around in the seat as you played the game. This was an attempt to make arcade games unique again but this sort of thing never really caught on enough to turn in a tidy profit and save arcades. Arcades today are more of a nostalgia thing

than a necessity.

(467) Sadie said she loves living in New Jersey because you can pop into the centre of New York whenever you want.

(468) The Police song Every Breath You Take closes Stranger Things 2 as the Flayer ominously lurks beyond our dimension and the Snow Ball dance. In the original script for this episode it was planned to close the episode with the Phil Collins song In the Air Tonight.

(469) Sadie said she is happiest spending time with her family.

(470) Stranger Things was originally going to be called Montauk and set by the coast. When these plans were abandoned they had to come up with a brand new title. The titles they considered were The Rift, The Nether, Sentinel, Flickers, The Keep, The Tesseract, and Wormhole. A title they nearly settled on was Indigo but Matt Duffer eventually came up with Stranger Things - which was inspired by the Stephen King story Needful Things.

(471) Sadie says she likes to 'toughen' up a flowery dress with some boots.

(472) Sadie said she constantly learns from watching other actors on a set.

(473) Sadie thinks that even if she hadn't become famous she'd still be the same person today. The only difference is that she'd probably have a lot less money!

(474) Sadie said she went through a lot of different phases as a teenager.

(475) Sadie said she is scared of clowns.

(476) Sadie said you shouldn't take life too seriously.

(477) 250 wigs were used during the production of Stranger Things 4. Sadie was one of the few actors who simply used her own hair!

(478) Sadie has appeared on the cover of Bello magazine.

(479) Sadie thinks it would be fun to see a Stranger Things spin-off show based on the character of Erica Sinclair.

(480) The finale of Stranger Things 3 features an unexpected duet when Suzie makes Dustin sing the theme song to The Neverending Story with her before she will divulge the Planck's constant numbers for the Russian code. Sadie and the other cast members only heard the duet when the reactions of their characters were shot. Their baffled reactions were therefore genuine.

(481) The horror is Stranger Things 4 is more graphic than we've seen before in the show thanks to Vecna's bone snapping antics. This is because the Duffers judged that young fans of Stranger Things who had grown-up with the show were now older.

(482) Broadway is a historic street in Manhattan, New York City, known for its theatres and musical productions. The term "Broadway" is also used to refer to the theatre industry and musical productions in New York City as a whole. The theatre district on Broadway is concentrated in Midtown Manhattan, primarily around Times Square.

(483) The first Broadway theatre, the Park Theater, opened in

1798.

(484) The Glass Castle, which Sadie acted in, is a 2017 drama film directed by Destin Daniel Cretton and based on Jeannette Walls' memoir of the same name.

(485) The 2016 film Chuck, which Sadie had a small part in, is a biopic of the boxer Chuck Wepner. Chuck Wepner was a heavyweight boxer in the sixties and seventies. Wepner was what you might call a fringe contender or a journeyman. He was tough but a notch below the best in the division. In 1975, Wepner was an unlikely challenger to world heavyweight champion Muhammad Ali and lasted to the 15th round. Wepner even had a small moment of glory when he stepped on Ali's foot and the resulting tumble was mistakenly scored as a knockdown for Wepner.

One person who watched the Ali-Wepner fight was a struggling young actor named Sylvester Stallone. The sight of this overmatched plucky clubfighter fighting Muhammad Ali inspired Stallone to write Rocky. Stallone also promised Wepner that he would give him a break in Hollywood and cast him in one of his films. Wepner auditioned for a part in Rocky II but was not given the part. Wepner had further cause for complaint when Rocky III featured Stallone fighting Hulk Hogan (as Thunderlips) in a boxer v wrestler contest. In 1976, Wepner had participated in a boxer v wrestler clash against André the Giant and even been thrown out of the ring (which Thunderlips also does to Rocky Balboa in Rocky III). Over the decades since Rocky came out, Wepner has attempted various legal actions which seek to claim that Rocky was based on his own life and that he was never given any credit for this. Stallone has never though confirmed that Rocky was based on Chuck Wepner - although clearly it was.

(486) Sadie has 230 lines as Max in Stranger Things 4. Only four other actors have more lines in this season.

(487) Sadie had 208 lines in Stranger Things 3 as Max. This ranked her eighth when it came to most lines in the season.

(488) The most lines that Sadie has enjoyed in a single episode of Stranger Things is 48 lines in Dear Billy.

(489) The Michael Myers mask that Max wears at Halloween in Stranger Things 2 makes an amusing appearance in Stranger Things 4 when Eddie Munson uses it to disguise himself at the trailer park.

(490) Sadie said she still gives her skateboard an occasional whirl from time to time. She probably has a bit less time for skateboarding these days.

(491) Sadie said she is very proud of the way that her friend Millie Bobby Brown has built a beauty business empire away from acting.

(492) The cast of The Whale all stayed in an old manor house when they shot the film. This is the house that Sadie said was a bit nippy because the heating malfunctioned.

(493) Sadie said it can be a bit of a grind sometimes doing press junkets and promotion. This is just an unavoidable part of the acting industry - you have to go out and sell the product you've made. It probably gets a bit wearing being asked the same questions over and over again!

(494) Sadie has been featured in Flaunt magazine.

(495) Before she did The Whale, Sadie had never been to any

film festivals.

(496) Sadie said she felt quite sad when The Whale finished shooting. "Saying goodbye was weirdly emotional for me. And I don't know why, but especially after filming those final scenes, I feel like I felt a really deep connection to Ellie, which I don't think I'd ever really felt on any project that I'd ever done."

(497) Sadie said she doesn't really use products on her hair much.

(498) Sadie said that she likes using headbands.

(499) Sadie said she sometimes wears more than one fragrance to have a blend of scents.

(500) It was hairstylist Tommy Buckett who cut Sadie's hair into a short mullet for a film role. Buckett said he worried that people might hate him for chopping off Sadie's long hair!

(501) Sadie said that stylists have told her never to colour or dye her hair lest it doesn't go back to its natural red!

(502) Sadie chose a strange place to unveil her shorter hair. It was a photo taken in the cockpit of a Croatia Airlines flight!

(503) Sadie attended a Taylor Swift concert in Los Angeles in August 2023. Taylor Swift gave Sadie a mention during the concert.

(504) Sadie said she used to hate her freckles when she was a kid but now she loves them.

(505) When she went to the SAG awards in 2018, Sadie wore a

Chanel Fine Jewelry brooch in her hair.

(506) Sadie said that with her acting career she tries not to 'overthink' things and prefers to go with her instincts.

(507) Sadie said that a turtleneck top is her secret tip for staying warmer when it is a bit chilly.

(508) Sadie and the other cast members had to have an hour long car journey each day to shoot the scenes at Gwinnett Place Mall in Stranger Things 3. They said this journey got slightly tiresome in the end.

(509) Sadie said she doesn't really believe in ghosts.

(510) Celebrities like Sadie can make a lot of money from Instagram because they are paid to do sponsored posts promoting brands.

(511) In 2022 it was calculated that Sadie ranked fourth when it came to money made on Instagram by Stranger Things cast members. Millie Bobby Brown was way out in front with Finn Wolfhard second and Noah Schnapp third. It is believed though that Sadie has leapfrogged Finn and Noah since then thanks to Stranger Things 4 (where she had an expanded role), The Whale, and her Taylor Swift music film. Sadie's star was definitely on the rise in 2022 and beyond.

(512) Sadie said she owns far too many pairs of shoes because she can never bring herself to throw anything away.

(513) Sadie said if she has a comfy jumper or pair of jeans that she likes she will often end up wearing them each day.

(514) Sadie said she is constantly baking at home in an

attempt to improve her cooking skills.

(515) Sadie says she never really goes on holiday because whenever she makes plans for one there is a schedule conflict with her acting.

(516) Sadie said she doesn't look at fashion stuff on TikTok. She prefers to watch baking or comedy clips.

(517) Millie Bobby Brown said she always makes sure her trailer is next to Sadie's trailer on the Stranger Things set.

(518) Although the character of Will Byers is sensitive and shy, Sadie says that Noah Schnapp is the loudest person in the Stranger Things cast behind the scenes.

(519) Sadie has expressed her love for vintage fashion.

(520) Sadie has talked about the importance of balancing work and personal life to maintain a healthy lifestyle.

(521) Sadie said she found music concerts a bit intimidating when she was younger but now she enjoys them more now.

(522) Sadie is a fan of Jane Austen novels.

(523) Sadie said that playing Max in Stranger Things has had a positive impact on her life as the character has empowered her and helped her gain confidence.

(524) There were a lot stories that Sadie was going to be in Tim Burton's Beetlejuice sequel but these didn't turn out to be true. The original Beetlejuice was one of the films that helped make Sadie's Stranger Things co-star Winona Ryder a star. Winona will be appearing in the sequel.

(525) Taylor Swift wrote a tribute to Sadie in Entertainment Weekly. The opening paragraph went like this - 'Sadie Sink is a remarkable presence on screen, on stage, and on set. While watching the monitors during the filming of the short film we made together, I often found myself transfixed by the effortlessness and complexity of her performance. Scratch that, because it didn't feel like a performance at all. Her grief, her hope, her loss — it all felt real. I often tell people that Sadie's face is so transparent, you can even see the thoughts she almost has. After over a decade of work, as the internet would say, this year "Sadie Sink's rent was due."

She helped bring "Running Up That Hill" by Kate Bush back into the cultural spotlight with a harrowing performance as Max Mayfield on Stranger Things season 4. Max's conflicted sorrow, regret, and resentment was potent and piercing in her portrayal, a slow burn that simmered with intensity. Even when despondent, Max's fury was palpable from beneath layers of hurt. It was an evolutionary turn for the character, helmed gracefully and tastefully by an artist who knows how to extensively prepare and fully commit.'

(526) Sadie was in the stage show Annie for 18 months in all.

(527) Sadie said that when you are a child actor in the stage show Annie they have a maximum height limit. Once you get taller than this you are considered too old to play an orphan!

(528) Sadie said that although it was awkward at the time she can look back and laugh now about her kissing scene with Caleb McLaughlin at the end of Stranger Things 2.

(529) Sadie was fifteen when she did her first red carpet event. This was obviously Stranger Things 2.

(530) Although it will be sad to say goodbye, Sadie thinks that Stranger Things is ending at the right time. If the show went on for too long a number of people might get a bit fed-up with it in the end - sort of like what happened with The Walking Dead. It is best to leave people wanting a bit more rather than make them feel as if they got too much.

(531) A special cloth grid was put in the Starcourt Mall on Stranger Things 3 set to block out daylight for certain scenes. This was so that scenes supposed to be set at night could be shot during the day without any sunshine infiltrating the mall.

(532) Sadie said she only had a few hours to look at the script before the first table read for The Whale.

(533) Kyle Lambert was hired to produce the posters for Stranger Things. His brief was to replicate hand painted film artwork found in vintage movie posters from the 1980s.

(534) Sadie has been on The Today Show. The Today Show is an American morning talk and news show that airs on NBC. It has been on the air since 1952.

(535) The Hawkins Department of Energy building in Stranger Things is really the former Georgia Mental Health Institute (now Emory University Briarcliff Campus, Atlanta).

(536) Sadie thinks that time has flown since she became famous. "2023 doesn't seem like a real year — that was when my credit card was going to expire and I was like, 'That's not real!'"

(537) In the promotion for Stranger Things 2, the new character of Max Mayfield was described in the following way

- "Max, a tough and confident girl whose appearance, behavior and pursuits seem more typical of boys than of girls in this era. She has a complicated history and is generally suspicious of those around her."

(538) Sadie is often listening to music through headphones when she's 'papped' by the media out and about.

(539) Sadie says that a season of Stranger Things is such a long shoot that you go a bit doollaly after about six months and can't even remember where you are!

(540) Max Mayfield ranks eighth when it comes to Stranger Things characters with the most overall screen time. That isn't bad considering Max wasn't in season one.

(541) The Duffer Brothers said they did a very wide casting search before they picked Sadie to play Max Mayfield.

(542) Sadie has some Ética jeans.

(543) The Duffer Brothers said it was just a coincidence that so many of the kids in Stranger Things have Broadway backgrounds.

(544) Sadie is fond of Dr. Martens boots.

(545) Netflix partnered with Madrid to produce a replica of Max's Stranger Things skateboard to purchase.

(546) Millie Bobby Brown said she loved the Taylor Swift music film with Sadie. "The 10-minute version of All Too Well changed my life. The film? Sadie? I just sat there and cried, practically," said Millie.

(547) Looper ranked Max Mayfield as the eighth most likeable character in Stranger Things. Eleven and Steve Harrington topped the poll.

(548) Sadie wore an Alexander McQueen dress on Late Night with Seth Meyers.

(549) The Duffers were always adamant throughout the planning and writing that Stranger Things would have a very limited number of episodes. They didn't want their show to ever feel like it was treading water or spreading its premise out too thinly.

(550) Sadie described shooting the Stranger Things 4 episode Dear Billy as emotionally exhausting.

(551) Sadie said she feels very lucky and blessed as an actor to get paid to do something she loves.

(552) Sadie says that jeg lag is an unavoidable consequence of attending European film festivals.

(553) Sadie has sometimes been seen wearing spectacles.

(554) O'Dessa, a new film which Sadie is acting in, is described as a 'rock musical'.

(555) O'Dessa was shot in Croatia.

(556) Sadie said she enjoys the classic Disney films.

(557) The Stranger Things set decorators trawl through dozens of thrift stores and garage sales to look for items that might be authentic to the middle America of the 1980s.

(558) Sadie said it took a while before she had the courage and confidence to express her opinions on a set when shooting a scene.

(559) The junkyard sequence in Stranger Things 2 was shot in a real junkyard.

(560) Sadie said she would never wear anything too crazy on the red carpet because she wouldn't want to stand out too much and be the centre of attention.

(561) Sadie said she doesn't like fragrances which are too overpowering.

(562) Sadie said that when you are an actor you often end up living out of a suitcase.

(563) Sadie said that it was a bit overwhelming the first time people started asking her for autographs and photos but she's more used to it now.

(564) Sadie said that if you are an actor you have to learn how to cope with boredom because you spend a lot of time doing nothing while you wait for scenes and shots to be set up.

(565) Sadie is a fan of the reality show Queer Eye. She said she was 'starstruck' when she met some of the stars of the show.

(566) Sadie said she loves the music and fashion of the 1970s and wouldn't mind living in that decade.

(567) Sadie said if she hadn't become an actor she would have liked to become a lawyer.

(568) Sadie says that stage acting is more technical than

screen acting because your performance is geared towards a live audience.

(569) Sadie said that being cast in Stranger Things changed the whole course of her life in an incredible way.

(570) When she was in the stage show Annie, Sadie often had to do eight performances a week. It was a tough schedule for one so young.

(571) Sadie said she was terrified when she appeared in The Americans because she'd never been in a television or film studio before.

(572) Sadie said that Broadway was good training because it teaches you to learn your lines and give a consistent performance.

(573) The production of a new season of Stranger Things is an increasingly complex and lengthy operation. Even when the actors have filmed their scenes and gone home it still takes months to complete the digital effects.

(574) Some Stranger Things fans believe that when the screen turns upside down right at the end of Stranger Things 2 the cars seem to take on an anachronistic quality.

(575) Sadie said that working with (director) Stephen Daldry, (writer) Peter Morgan, and Helen Mirren on The Audience was fantastic acting training for her as a kid.

(576) One theory for why the Duffers got over a dozen rejections when they first tried to pitch Stranger Things is that there had been a number of underwhelming television shows and miniseries based on the stories of Stephen King.

The prospect of another show heavily inspired by Stephen king evidently wasn't an appealing prospect to many executives.

(577) Sadie said that one of the reasons she went back to school after Broadway is that a director told her you need some life experiences to be a good actor. Sadie felt that going to school was a pretty important life experience.

(578) Sadie said that her Stranger Things 2 auditions were a lot of fun to do.

(579) On the end of Stranger Things, Sadie said - "What's it going to feel like knowing I will never play this character again—this character who has set my life on a course I never thought it would go on? To never play that character again will be a very sad day."

(580) 'Stranger Things: The Experience' - an immersive experience based on the show - opened in a number of cities in 2022. In the experience you get to rescue Max from Vecna and can also visit Family Video and Scoops Ahoy. The experience has drawn positive reviews in the media.

(581) Sadie says she would like to play challenging and diverse characters in the future. She would hate to do the same thing all the time.

(582) Sadie says she would like to do more theatre work again one day.

(583) Sadie said one of her favourite scenes to play in Stranger Things 4 was when Max read out the letter at Billy's grave in Dear Billy.

(584) Although the renovations and machines were removed after shooting on Stranger Things 2 ended, the Palace Arcade stripes painted on the side of the building are still there. This has made the building a popular place for Stranger Things fans to have their photograph taken.

(585) When they embarked on season two, the producers on Stranger Things were advised by the Games of Thrones crew on how how to maintain secrecy on a high profile television production. Big shows like Stranger Things have to do their best to avoid leaks and spoilers.

(586) There is a lot of singing on the Stranger Things set - which is probably not surprising given the musical stage background of several cast members.

(587) The chapter titles at the start of each episode of Stranger Things are to make it feel like you are digesting a Stephen King novel.

(588) Sadie has been on the cover of Backstage magazine.

(589) The raptors in Jurassic Park were a big influence on the DemoDogs in season two of Stranger Things.

(590) Sadie said Fear Street 2 was quite scary to make with all the peril and danger which abounded for her character.

(591) Georgia made a great production base for Stranger Things because the area had an eclectic mix of scenery from gorges to forests to Spielbergian towns.

(592) Most of the big sequences in Stranger Things are planned by use of storyboards and models before they are actually shot.

(593) In a poll, Stranger Things came top out of Netflix shows which can be enjoyed by the whole family.

(594) The parents and siblings of the children in the Stranger Things cast were a regular presence on the set during the early seasons.

(595) Sadie is a fan of Jodie Foster. Jodie Foster, like Sadie, began her career as a child actor.

(596) The production designers on Stranger Things say that when they find a street they want to use in the show there are three main things they have to do. They have to put in period accurate cars and mail boxes and also remove any modern satellite dishes.

(597) Sadie has been praised for her strong work ethic and dedication to her craft.

(598) Sadie has said that she hopes to inspire young girls who have acting and performing aspirations.

(599) Sadie said that if she has a bag that she likes she will usually end up using it each day for a month or two rather than constantly change bags simply for fashion or brand reasons.

(600) The design of Vecna in Stranger Things 4 patently owes something to The Gill-Man in Creature from the Black Lagoon. Creature from the Black Lagoon (what a great name for a film) was released in 1954 and directed by Jack Arnold from a screenplay by Harry Essex.

(601) Sadie said that when you have a big red carpet event looming you can sometimes get into a panic trying to work

out what to wear. That's why celebrities pay stylists to choose outfits for them!

(602) Sadie said that when she joined the cast of Stranger Things she was amazed and impressed by how relaxed and calm the other kids in the show were about their sudden fame and all the attention they were getting.

(603) Cinechat wrote of Fear Street 2 - 'Everything about this film feels like a step up from Part One, and that's definitely true for the blood and gore. It takes over 40 minutes for us to see a killing, but once this gets started it doesn't stop until the very end, with a poignant and rather harrowing final scene with the two sisters. There's also a pleasantly surprising twist towards the end that while it doesn't have a major impact in terms of the overall plot, it really worked in subverting everything we as a viewer had been thinking for the past 90 minutes.'

(604) Shawn Levy is a producer and director on Stranger Things. Sadie used to be roommates and best friends with Levy's daughter Sophie. Sadie and Sophie later deleted one another from their social media - which obviously suggests they had a falling out.

(605) The Americans, which Sadie appeared in as a kid, is a television drama series that aired from 2013 to 2018. It follows the lives of two Soviet intelligence officers, Elizabeth and Philip Jennings, who pose as an American married couple living in suburban Washington, D.C., during the 1980s Cold War era. They work for the KGB and carry out espionage and sabotage missions while balancing their covert activities with the challenges of raising their two children.

(606) Sadie has appeared on Carpool Karaoke with James

Corden.

(607) Sadie appeared on Beyond Stranger Things in 2017. This was basically a show on Netflix which interviewed the cast and supplied some behind the scenes info.

(608) Sadie is a big fan of the song Savior Complex by Phoebe Bridgers.

(609) Sadie has appeared on the cover of Cool Magazine in France.

(610) When she joined the cast of Stranger Things, Sadie had a lot of sleepovers with Millie Bobby Brown.

(611) Sadie has appeared on the cover of Who What Wear Magazine.

(612) Sadie has done a photoshoot for S Moda Magazine. S Moda Magazine is a Spanish fashion and lifestyle magazine.

(613) Stranger Things is a perfect example of how important casting and characters are in a television show. Stranger Things has wonderfully memorable characters who you can't imagine being played by any other actors.

(614) Dylan O'Brien, who starred opposite Sadie in the Taylor Swift music video, is probably best known for his lead role in the Maze Runner films.

(615) When she was a child actor on Broadway, Sadie would often not get out of the theatre until midnight.

(616) Out of the core Stranger Things 'kids' (Sadie, Millie, Gaten, Finn, Noah, Caleb), Sadie is the second oldest after

Caleb McLaughlin. Noah Schnapp and Millie Bobby Brown are the two youngest. Millie and Noah were born in 2004 whereas the others (apart from Caleb - born in 2001) were born in 2002.

(617) Sadie has appeared on The Broadway.com Show. The Broadway.com Show is a weekly web series that provides behind-the-scenes access to the world of Broadway.

(618) Sadie said she finds our technology obsessed age a bit annoying sometimes. "There is nothing worse than going to dinner with your friends or your family and you're trying to make conversation and everyone's head is just buried in their phones and you are just looking around. It happened to me once and all of my friends were like buried in their phones and I just looked around and I was like, 'Wow, is this really what it has come to?' I can't even talk to my friends!"

(619) Sadie said is not the sort of person who is always glued to her phone or constantly scrolling.

(620) Sadie doesn't have any formal acting training. She never went to drama school or anything like that. Her foundation was Texas community theatre and then of course Broadway.

(621) Sadie said she loved Joseph Quinn as Eddie Munson in Stranger Things 4.

(622) Sadie has starred in a Givenchy beauty campaign.

(623) Sadie is a fan of the actress Saoirse Ronan.

(624) Sadie said she is glad that Broadway was her entry point into the 'industry' - as opposed to Hollywood.

(625) Sadie said she got the part of Max in Stranger Things the day after doing a 'chemistry' read with Gaten Matarazzo and Caleb McLaughlin.

(626) Sadie said that she loved working on The Audience because it felt very spontaneous and fresh with each new performance.

(627) Joe Keery (who plays Steve) said the kids in the cast banished him from their Stranger Things chat group during season two because he was too old to be a member!

(628) The fog smoked hell dimension of spooky decayed corridors the Cenobites in Clive Barker's Hellraiser inhabit was an influence on the Upside Down in Stranger Things.

(629) Sadie said that Taylor Swift gave her plenty of useful advice about 'navigating' the entertainment industry.

(630) Among the subjects Sadie took at school were calculus and psychology.

(631) Sadie said she once wore a Miu Miu sweater to school.

(632) Sadie said that after working with Helen Mirren on The Audience she came to the conclusion that British people swear a lot!

(633) Despite their exploits in Stranger Things, Sadie, Natalia Dyer, Charlie Heaton, and Priah Ferguson have all said they are not horror fans and don't watch horror shows or movies in real life.

(634) Sadie had to submit an audition tape for the stage show Annie. She was hired as an understudy at first.

(635) Sadie said she knew Stranger Things had a big fanbase after the first season was so popular but she only realised how huge that fanbase was when she actually joined the show.

(636) Gwinnett Place Mall was perfect for the Starcourt Mall in Stranger things 3 because it had two levels. This meant there would be plenty of room to rig up cameras and move them around. The Duffers instructed that the mall design in season three should have a Gap, Scoops Ahoy (obviously), and some sort of photo studio (for the Max and Eleven montage), but they left the rest of the stores to be decided by the production team.

(637) Regarding fame, Sadie said - "It's such a weird and specific situation that the Strangers Things cast and I are all in because the world knows who our characters are but we're still trying to figure out who we are as people."

(638) Sadie said that when she left Broadway and went back to school it was actually quite nice to take a break from the responsibility and pressure of acting and performing.

(639) Sadie said actors are naturally quite insecure and always worried that they won't get that next job.

(640) Sadie said of Stranger Things ending - "It feels like a graduation of sorts. We've all been on [Stranger Things] long enough that we've developed these individual career paths, but the show is a home base. I'm not going to lie, losing that is going to be heartbreaking, but I think we're all in a good place to do so."

(641) Sadie said that Winona Ryder (who obviously plays Joyce Byers in the show) has been a very kind and wise anchor and mentor for the younger cast members on the Stranger Things

set.

(642) Shawn Levy said that getting clearance to use famous songs on Stranger Things is no picnic because they don't have the budget to get most of the ones they want to use.

(643) Michelle Andrea Adams was the stunt double for Sadie in Stranger Things 4. Michelle has also done stunts on shows like Cobra Kai and The Walking Dead.

(644) The first person to play Annie on Broadway was Andrea McArdle. This was in 1977.

(645) Sarah Jessica Parker was one of the first kids to play Annie on Broadway. She later became best known for Sex and the City. Trivia you will never need - Shelley Bruce, another early Annie star on Broadway, later appeared in the cultish 1981 slasher film The Burning. Shelley Bruce played the character named Tiger in The Burning. So, Sadie wasn't the first Annie star who went on to appear in a horror film!

(646) In an episode of The Simpsons, Homer watched a Stranger Things parody called Odder Stuff.

(647) Sadie said that when she gets a new script she uses her 'gut instincts' to decide if it is right for her.

(648) The boxing biopic Chuck that Sadie had a small part in had an amazing cast. It featured Liev Schreiber, Elizabeth Moss, Ron Pearlman, Naomi Watts, and Michael Rapaport.

(649) Sadie has had to wear a lot of corduroy in period pieces Stranger Things and Fear Street!

(650) Showbiz Junkies wrote of the film Dear Zoe - 'Sadie Sink

does a phenomenal job as Tess, a teenager forced to face the sudden loss of someone she loved deeply and who emerges stronger from the experience. Tess is flawed and relatable; she doesn't always make the right choices. Sink's performance allows us to live each of the heartbreaks with Tess, and also celebrate the moments when Tess allows herself to just breathe.'

(651) Sadie loves Prada shoes without heels.

(652) Sadie has been called a Scream Queen. Scream Queen is a term used to describe an actress who frequently appears in horror films. Some well-known Scream Queens include Jamie Lee Curtis and Linnea Quigley.

(653) Sadie said that Fear Street 2 is the most physical role she has had to play so far.

(654) Sadie said she wasn't allowed to watch horror films when she was growing up.

(655) Sadie said her first experience of horror films was secretly watching some at her cousin's house. She said one of the first horror films she can remember watching is John Carpenter's Halloween. This is nice symmetry given that Stranger Things is very influenced by John Carpenter.

(656) Sadie said one horror film she did love was 2019's Ready or Not. The story in Ready or Not revolves around a young bride, Grace, who marries into the wealthy and eccentric Le Domas family. On her wedding night, she is coerced into participating in a family tradition: playing a game chosen by the family at random. What starts as a harmless game of hide-and-seek quickly turns into a deadly survival game as Grace realises that her in-laws have sinister intentions.

(657) Surprisingly, Stranger Things is not the Netflix show that has clocked up the most viewing hours by streamers. That title goes to The Squid Game. The Squid Game is a South Korean survival drama television series created by Hwang Dong-hyuk. The show follows a group of struggling individuals who participate in a mysterious survival competition known as "The Squid Game" for a chance to win a substantial cash prize.

(658) Sadie said she had no idea that there would be so many stunts and so much action in Fear Street 2. She said it was great fun to do though.

(659) Sadie is a fan of the music themed drama film Whiplash.

(660) Sadie said she was very happy that Stranger Things 4 dealt with how Max was affected by the end of Stranger Things 3 - where her brother Billy died. Sadie said she would have been disappointed if this was glossed over.

(661) Sadie is a fan of the singer Maggie Rogers.

(662) There are a few goofs in Stranger Things 2 when it comes to science. There is, for example, a periodic table in the school which contains some elements that hadn't been discovered in 1984.

(663) Sadie is a fan of The Weeknd. Abel Makkonen Tesfaye, known professionally as the Weeknd, is a Canadian singer, songwriter, and record producer.

(664) Sadie said that one of the things that drew her to Fear Street was the representation of gay characters.

(665) Sadie is a fan of the rock band The Scissors.

(666) Stranger Things co-creator Matt Duffer said that you can tell very quickly if child actors are any good or not. The Duffers wanted authentic regular kids and were wary of casting kids who seemed too polished, confident or slick.

(667) The moment in Stranger things 2 where Steve wakes up in the car (which is being driven by Max) after his pounding at the hands of Billy and groggily says Nancy's name was apparently improvised by Joe Keery.

(668) A number of actors have come forward and said they auditioned for Stranger Things but didn't get cast. To give some examples, Chase Stokes, star of the Netflix show Outer Banks, said he auditioned to play Steve Harrington in Stranger Things but messed up his audition by forgetting most of his lines. Bridgerton actress Nicola Coughlan said she unsuccessfully auditioned for the part of Robin in Stranger Things 3. However, at the time of writing, not a single actress has come forward and said they unsuccessfully auditioned to be Max Mayfield. It seems then that Sadie was always in pole position for this role.

(669) Sadie won a Best Actor award at the Woods Hole Film Festival for Dear Zoe.

(670) Sadie once said she was scared of dolphins. That's seems a strange thing to be scared of!

(671) Decider wrote of Fear Street Part 2: 1978 - 'In many ways, Ziggy from Fear Street feels like a side-quest story for Max from Stranger Things—that time Max Mayfield was born 10 years earlier, got sent to summer camp, and also had an older sister. Like Max, Ziggy comes from a broken family and doesn't hesitate to tell everyone she doesn't agree with where to shove it. But unlike Stranger Things, Fear Street is rated R,

meaning Sink, who is 19, can actually swear. (It's also very violent and bloody, so do keep that in mind if you're only watching the horror movie for Sink.)'

(672) You can hear a blast of Maurice Jarre's score from Peter Weir's 1985 film Witness during the antenna raising scenes in Stranger Things 3.

(673) Sadie only spend a few days working on Fear Street Part Three: 1666. It was the second film where she had the biggest part.

(674) Sadie said she would live to play Carole King in a biopic. Carole King is an American singer-songwriter, pianist, and composer who is known for her contributions to the popular music industry. King wrote, among other songs, Will You Love Me Tomorrow and The Loco-Motion.

(675) The first Stranger Things episode that Sadie appeared in was titled MADMAX. MADMAX works as an effective scene setter and enjoyably slips us back into the world of Hawkins and its characters. The episode captures much of the essence and Stranger Things residue of the first season and so feels more like a continuation of the story than a new season. If you watch season one and MADMAX back to back there doesn't feel like there is much difference in tone or atmosphere. The kids don't seem to have aged much and that retro synth score still manages to charm during the softer scenes and supply a pounding backdrop to the action or tension when it arrives.

(676) Sadie is a fan of David Bowie. The Man who Sold the World is her favourite Bowie song.

(677) Sadie said the physicality of Fear Street was great preparation for Stranger Things 4.

(678) Sadie says that Brenham, where she grew up, was not a very arty town. Sadie says that it was more of a football town because everyone was sports mad.

(679) Sadie lives in New York. It's a short hop to her parents in New Jersey but a much longer hop to Atlanta where Stranger Things is made. What with photoshoots and interviews too, Sadie clocks up a fair few air miles.

(680) The Duffer Brothers and Shawn Levy said that not every alleged homage or Easter egg in Stranger Things is deliberate. They say that occasionally they are even accused of doing a homage to a movie that they haven't even heard of!

(681) Sadie has to do a lot of Zoom interviews promoting her film projects and Stranger Things.

(682) The script for the season three finale was thirty pages longer than any other episode in Stranger Things 3. This is because there was so much action and mayhem to describe.

(683) Sadie wore Prada to the Fear Street premiere.

(684) The production designers on Stranger Things 3 had a nice stroke of luck when they found a folder that included many photographs of Gwinnett Place Mall (as it was in the eighties). This was a big help in turning it into the Starcourt Mall and making it look period authentic to 1985.

(685) Sadie said that she does her own dishes and laundry at home. She isn't the sort of celebrity who has housekeepers and flunkies!

(686) The 'chapters' of Stranger Things are shrewdly engineered to end with cliffhangers and revelations so that

you must quickly move onto the next episode.

(687) Screen Rant wrote of the film Dear Zoe - 'Sadie Sink has shown that she is a force to be reckoned with over the last five years. From her first appearance as Max Mayfield on Netflix's Stranger Things to her most recent acclaimed performance in Darren Aronofsky's The Whale, the young actress shows no limits to where her talents can take her. Sadie's latest show-stopping performance sees her bearing the heavy emotional weight of the loss of a loved one. Based on the 2005 American novel of the same name, Dear Zoe captures a sincere glimpse of grief when the surrounding world deals with its own problems. Director Gren Wells crafts a tender, yet narratively unbalanced film that accentuates the gift that is Sadie Sink's talent.'

(688) Season one of Stranger Things was designed to have an autumn atmosphere. This is why you see a lot of orange. Season two was more saturated and blue. Season three is probably best described as the neon season. Season four had a lot of different locations so it had various moods and looks.

(689) When she was a little kid, Sadie appeared in a commercial for Stony Brook Children's Hospital. She played a little girl about to have an appendix operation.

(690) Sadie has appeared on SiriusXM's Entertainment Weekly Radio to promote Stranger Things.

(691) Max Mayfield uses Sony Nova 45 Headphones with her Walkman in Stranger Things 4.

(692) Max Mayfield has a Herschel Backpack in Stranger Things 2.

(693) Sadie was only in one episode of The Americans. She wasn't a regular or recurring cast member.

(694) Stranger Things costume designer Kim Wilcox said that Sadie and the kids (as they were then) in the cast never complained about what their characters were given to wear. "They don't bring in their high fashion wants into the room because they know that's not what their characters are about. They're very professional. I've worked with a lot of very young actors in my career and these are some of the most talented, most fun, most professional actors I've ever worked with — at any age."

(695) Sadie thinks the appeal of Stranger Things is that it is essentially a coming of age story.

(696) A young woman named Jamie Helton has been the body double for Sadie in Stranger Things. In the earlier seasons the kids had body doubles for some shots because they were only allowed to work a limited amount of hours. They obviously don't show the face of the body doubles onscreen - hence the term 'body' double!

(697) The 'Zone' (a restricted area of great mystery) in the 1979 science fiction film Stalker by Andrei Tarkovsky was a big influence on the design of the Upside Down in Stranger Things.

(698) Sadie said that when she was a little kid one of her ambitions was to get on Master Chef Junior. Master Chef Junior is a reality television cooking competition show that features talented young chefs between the ages of 8 and 13.

(699) Sadie and the other Stranger Things kids appeared on the cover of Cinemanía Magazine in 2019. Cinemanía

Magazine is a Spanish film magazine that covers both national and international cinema.

(700) Mashable wrote of Fear Street 2 - 'Meticulously written and performed by an obviously passionate cast, Fear Street's second outing earns its best moments by playing smart. Fiery performances by Sink and Rudd help underscore the film's originality, offering unique portrayals of recognizable characters you've never met quite like this. Thanks to Part 2, the stakes of Fear Street are higher, the mystery of Shadyside is deeper.'

(701) It is fair to say there was something of a critical backlash against The Whale when the reviews came out. A number of reviewers felt that the depiction of the central character Charlie was distasteful and simplistic in that it (in their view) portrayed overweight people as sad, lonely, and sort of disgusting.

(702) Slate.Com wrote of The Whale - 'Is The Whale, at its core, an exercise in fatphobia? As a critic and viewer who is not a member of the plus-size community, I'm not certain it's my place to answer. The movie's defects strike me more as lapses in tone and taste than as an error in the choice of subject matter: It's possible to imagine a film about the same subject that didn't turn its main character into a spectacle for pity, or one that cast an actor closer to Charlie's weight in the lead, rather than just a heavyset one in a padded suit. It's also possible to imagine some viewers, whatever their size, finding beauty and empathy in Aronofsky's portrait of a soul in freefall. And certainly Fraser—who plays Charlie as a wonderfully specific individual, with his own deep character flaws along with a tender heart and a sly sense of humor—goes a long way toward humanizing a character who could easily be nothing but a confluence of leaden metaphors. Given

the Academy's love for roles that require extreme physical self-transformation, it may well be that Fraser ends up winning a Best Actor award for The Whale. (He's already widely considered the favorite.) If so, he will join Joaquin Phoenix in a rare pantheon that should perhaps become an Oscar category all its own: best performance in a terrible movie.'

(703) There have been a number of Stranger Things pop up bars around the world.

(704) Sadie said that one of her big regrets is that she never appeared in a play or musical production at school.

(705) Sadie has appeared on Live with Kelly and Mark. Live with Kelly and Mark is a talk show hosted by Kelly Ripa and Mark Consuelos.

(706) It took a week to shoot the sequence in the Stranger Things 3 episode The Sauna Test where Billy is trapped by the kids.

(707) Sadie says she is not the sort of person who will buy something purely for the sake of it.

(708) Sadie said she was very excited when she became old enough to vote in elections.

(709) Sadie hopes that more and more people will become vegetarians and vegans.

(710) Sadie said - "The thing about being successful meaning you're famous, I don't think that is true. I personally feel like I am successful in other areas of life that don't have anything to do with acting. I am a big sister; I am a daughter; I am a friend;

I am more than just an actor."

(711) Sadie is a fan of Tina Fey's book Bossypants. Tina Fey is an American actress, comedian, writer, and producer.

(712) Sadie didn't miss out on a financial bonanza by not not being in season one of Stranger Things because the kids in the show reportedly only got about $20,000 an episode at the start. Netflix had no idea if the show would be popular or not so they obviously weren't going to go crazy with the salaries. That's all changed now. The salaries on Stranger Things 5 are liable to be eye-watering.

(713) Some people have suggested that All Too Well: The Short Film is really about Taylor Swift's relationship with the actor Jake Gyllenhaal. Taylor Swift dated Gyllenhaal for about three months when she was 20. Gyllenhaal is nine years older than Swift - which is similar to the age gap between Sadie and All Too Well co-star Dylan O'Brien.

(714) Jake Gyllenhaal responded to claims All Too Well: The Short Film was about him by saying - "It has nothing to do with me. It's about her relationship with her fans. It is her expression. Artists tap into personal experiences for inspiration, and I don't begrudge anyone that."

(715) The villain of Stranger Things 2 is the Mind Flayer - an unspecified big boss of the Upside Down. The manifestation of the creature is visually inspired by electric storms and volcanoes. The Duffers said that Voldemort in Harry Potter and the stories of Clive Barker were an influence on the Mind Flayer. The Flayer is a horror that can't be readily explained. The Mind Flayer is also clearly inspired by Lovecraft's cosmic entity Cthulhu.

(716) Sadie owns some Converse sneakers.

(717) Sadie attended the 2017 Humane Society of the United States to the Rescue! New York Gala at Cipriani 42nd Street in New York City in 2017.

(718) Sadie likes Alo Yoga caps.

(719) Sadie said the cast of Stranger Things get to watch the episodes before the public because Netflix add them to their streaming accounts two weeks prior to the premiere.

(720) Sadie says she enjoys visiting the seaside and being by the ocean.

(721) Centipede, one of the games in the Palace Arcade in Stranger Things 2, was one of the first arcade coin-operated games to have a significant female player base.

(722) Sadie is a fan of Billie Eilish.

(723) In an article, Rolling Stone magazine rated Stranger Things the sixteenth greatest horror television show of all time. The top spot went to Twin Peaks.

(724) Film Threat wrote of the film Dear Zoe - 'Dear Zoe is carried by Sadie Sink, who does a great job as the narrator. She makes her character's transformation feel earned and not just a plot point.'

(725) Sadie is a fan of the sitcom Schitt's Creek. She said she used to watch this to relax while shooting Fear Street 2.

(726) When the third season of Stranger Things was released early for press reviews, journalists had to agree not to discuss

any potential spoilers. They were given a list of seventeen plot points they were not permitted to mention in any advance review.

(727) Sadie said that real trusted friends are hard to find but she is lucky enough to have some.

(728) It took months to get permission from the Michael Jackson estate to use his song Thriller for the Stranger Things 2 trailer. Fifty other songs were considered but they were desperate to get the use of Thriller and so persisted. It was worth the effort. What they REALLY wanted was the narration on the song by Vincent Price. This gave the Stranger Things 2 trailer the perfect Halloween atmosphere.

(729) Sadie said it sometimes crazy filming Fear Street 2 because quite often she would be shooting some scene at 3am covered in fake blood!

(730) Although it is an anachronism for the arcade machines in Stranger Things 2 to have LCD screens (as opposed to cathode ray tube monitors) it was probably unavoidable because cathode ray tube monitors are difficult to capture perfectly when shot on film.

(731) Sadie said she isn't too fond of heights.

(732) The Stranger Things kids played a lot of Monopoly filming the second season.

(733) Sadie is a fan of the singer-songwriter Lana Del Rey.

(734) Sadie said that making a new season of Stranger Things is sort of like going back to school. You meet up again with old friends and soon get back into the swing of things.

(735) Sadie said that The Mind Flayer was her favourite episode in Stranger Things 2.

(736) Sadie felt it was quite brave to have a foot of her hair chopped off for a film role because her long red hair is obviously a major defining feature.

(737) Sadie attended Ted Sarandos' 2018 Annual Netflix Emmy Nominee Toast. Millie Bobby Brown was also there.

(738) The premiere of Stranger Things 2 took place at the Regency Bruin Theatre in Los Angeles. Sadie was of course in attendance.

(739) Sadie has a Chiara Ferragni t-shirt.

(740) You can now buy a Sadie Sink themed Tote bag.

(741) Sadie was nineteen when she started shooting Stranger Things 4. Given that Max was in high school in the show this obviously meant that Sadie was a few years older than the character she was playing.

(742) The boxing biopic Chuck that Sadie had a small part in is also called The Bleeder. This is obviously a reference to the fact that the boxer Chuck Wepner used to get cut a lot in his fights.

(743) Sadie was in one episode of a kids TV show called Bounce. This was obviously before she was famous. Bounce is a magazine style show for children.

(744) The argument in the kitchen in All Too Well: The Short Film was improvised by Sadie and Dylan O'Brien.

(745) All Too Well: The Short Film had a limited release in some New York cinemas.

(746) Stranger Things clearly takes some inspiration from Super 8 - a 2011 science fiction film written and directed by JJ Abrams. Super 8 is set in the late 1970s and is a homage to Steven Spielberg films of the seventies and eighties (Spielberg even produced Super 8). Super 8 is about a bunch of kids in a small town who end up in the middle of a mystery when some sort of creature gets loose. The kids have walkie-talkies and are very inspired by the sort of kids you would see in Amblin films of the eighties.

(747) Sadie said she is inspired by the activism of Rowan Blanchard. Rowan Blanchard is an American actress, best known for her role as Riley Matthews on the Disney Channel series Girl Meets World.

(748) Taylor Swift appears at the end of All Too Well: The Short Film as an older version of Sadie's character. Taylor Swift is about twelve years older than Sadie.

(749) Sadie, alongside other Stranger Things cast members, has appeared on the cover of SFX magazine.

(750) Fear Street 2 earned a very healthy 87% on Rotten Tomatoes.

(751) All Too Well: The Short Film was nominated in five categories at the 2022 MTV Video Music Awards.

(752) Sadie has appeared on Total Request Live. Total Request Live (often abbreviated as TRL) was a television show on MTV that aired from 1998 to 2008. In 2017, MTV revived TRL with a new format, this time focusing more on social media and

digital content. Sadie was obviously in the revamped version because she hadn't even been born when the original show started!

(753) The io9 website wrote of Stranger Things 2 - 'If you liked season one, and pretty much everyone did, then you'll like this season just fine. Everything is turned up a bit, but the soul of Stranger Things remains what it was last season—a story about friendship, family, and giant piles of '80s nostalgia. Stranger Things had an almost impossible task when it came to following up on a first season that had near-universal acclaim. That it's still engaging, gorgeous looking, and smartly written is a truly impressive feat. The show didn't hit any reset buttons; it let every character grow and change, and it's just remarkable. This is a show growing naturally into itself and does everything to make the nine-hour commitment worth it.'

(754) According to online sources, Sadie only made about $25,000 an episode on Stranger Things 3. This seems - if true - a bit modest.

(755) Business Insider claimed that Sadie would be getting $7 million for Stranger Things 5 - which is a huge salary if true.

(756) When it comes to the salaries on Stranger Things 5, Sadie is said to be in the 'second tier' with the other youngsters. David Harbour and Winona Ryder are in tier one. Millie Bobby Brown is not in any tier because she has a 'ridiculously lucrative' contract with Netflix which includes Stranger Things and other projects (like the Enola Holmes franchise). Suffice to say, the cast of Stranger Things won't be short of a bob or two when their cheques from season five are cashed.

(757) Sadie said she needed a break after Stranger Things 4 to rest her mind and body.

(758) Sadie said there is no specific role she wants to play. She prefers to play it by ear and see what offers come in.

(759) Sadie has implied that after Stranger Things she would be a trifle wary of getting involved in a television show again because they usually involve long contracts. She would rather be a free agent and hopefully do some films.

(760) Eli and the Fear Street films were both Netflix productions. Netflix is obviously the company behind Stranger Things too. Sadie getting a part in The Whale was important because she was stepping outside the Netflix family and beginning to forge her own independent path.

(761) Sadie says the reason she keeps social media at arm's length is the negativity.

(762) Stranger Things 3 is the first season of the show where the children (as they were) now look more like teenagers.

(763) Sadie and the other kids in Stranger Things had to have duplicates of the bikes their characters rode in the show lest one should get damaged or stop working.

(764) The monsters in Stranger Things 3 can melt into a puddle and reassemble themselves. This is a homage to the liquid metal T-1000 in Terminator 2: Judgment Day.

(765) Sadie likes the fashions of the 1920s - or the 'roaring 20s' as they tend to be known.

(766) Sadie, as we've mentioned, likes vegan chicken and

waffles. It is pretty simple to make this. You just need vegan waffles and Quorn style vegan 'chicken' nuggets.

(767) There were 2,000 digital effects in Stranger Things 2.

(768) Since she became famous and started working with brands, Sadie has had to attend an awful lot of swanky fashion event dinners.

(769) There were 2,500 digital effects in Stranger Things 3.

(770) Sadie said she does work out to keep fit - although it isn't an obsession.

(771) The Lost Sister is the lowest rated episode of Stranger Things on IMBD. Luckily for Sadie she wasn't in that one!

(772) The mall in Stranger Things 3 is similar to the mall in Chopping Mall - a cheesy 1986 horror comedy directed by Jim Wynorski.

(773) Sadie did not go to college after school because she was too busy with her acting career.

(774) Sadie said she has read some Shakespeare but admits that she found it tough going.

(775) Sadie said in an interview that having millions of Instagram followers isn't important.

(776) Although she enjoys reading, Sadie said she doesn't read horror fiction.

(777) Sadie has appeared on the cover of ES Magazine. ES Magazine is a weekly lifestyle and entertainment magazine

distributed with the Evening Standard newspaper in London.

(778) Sadie said she got the lead in Annie because the kid who had the part left the show unexpectedly.

(779) Stranger Things director and producer Shawn Levy has a cameo in the All Too Well music as the father of Sadie's character. Levy actually started his career as an actor.

(780) The Duffers Brothers said that most of the executives who rejected Stranger Things were looking for more of a Twin Peaks type of show. Stranger Things, as a pitch concept, was sort of like Stephen King meets The Goonies - which definitely isn't very Twin Peaks.

(781) There is now inevitably Stranger Things Minecraft.

(782) Sadie has appeared on the cover of Girlfriend Magazine.

(783) Because she eats out quite often, Sadie has joked about becoming a food critic one day.

(784) Millie Bobby Brown was nervous about a new girl joining the cast of children in Stranger Things 2 in case they didn't get along. Happily, she quickly became friends with Sadie and these fears proved unfounded.

(785) Taylor Swift said that Sadie was the only person she had in mind for the All Too Well music film.

(786) The Audience received critical acclaim and won several awards, including the Olivier Award for Best New Play in 2013.

(787) The Guardian wrote of Fear Street 2 - 'Again, so much of what makes this work is an extraordinarily talented group of

young actors who take the silliness of the witch's curse and sell it with heartfelt conviction. There's not one dud in the largely untested ensemble cast.'

(788) The villain is Stranger Things 4 named Vecna by the kids. Vecna was a wizard in Dungeons & Dragons. The character is known as the God of Secrets. Vecna was first referenced in OD&D's third supplement, Eldritch Wizardry.

(789) Stranger Things 3 features something that has become a tradition in the show - the cabin siege. This is a common trope in movies from vintage westerns through to films like Straw Dogs and The Evil Dead. One of the classic siege films is George A Romero's Night of the Living Dead. In this seminal 1968 horror film, a small group of characters try to survive in an isolated farmhouse that is surrounded by flesh eating zombies.

(790) One of the reasons why Harry Potter was so successful is that eschews the modern world and technology and gives us heroes who have a simpler (if hardly trouble free) way of life where nature, history, and friendship is more important than what brand of phone you have. The world of Harry Potter, with steam trains, castles, myths and legends, midnight feasts, is timeless and anachronistic. A trip to Hogwarts is like going back in time to escape from the present. This is what gives Harry Potter that comfort blanket feel which charmed readers around the world. A trip to 1980s Hawkins with the characters of Stranger Things also has a cosy comfort blanket feeling for viewers - despite all the monsters and mayhem which inevitably abound. This, as much as anything, might explain why the show is so popular.

(791) Shawn Levy said it was surprisingly complex to obtain permission to use a Michael Myers mask in Stranger Things 2.

(792) A Stranger Things Upside Down Lego set was released in which you can flip the set upside down to experience either dimension. 'Fans of the global hit Netflix original series will appreciate the authentic details of this highly collectible LEGO® Stranger Things toy – 75810 The Upside Down. This sturdy, brick-built model can flip between the real world and The Upside Down. The design of the model's building instructions makes it a great shared building experience with friends and family. The Byers' house features Will's bedroom, the living room and the dining room. The Upside Down version of the house, from an alternate dimension, features all the rooms from the real-world model but with a dark, vine-covered, dilapidated look that fans will instantly recognize from the series. With 8 Stranger Things figures, each with its own accessories, this playset makes a great gift for Stranger Things fans who will love to build and display this model to show their passion for the series.'

(793) The comics and novels based on Stranger Things tend to be prequels or what you might describe as side stories. This is obviously so they don't clash with the ongoing narrative in the show. There seems to be an attempt to maintain some sort of continuity through the different mediums.

(794) Sadie is a fan of the film Pan's Labyrinth.

(795) Sadie's shorter haircut in 2023 was partly based on a haircut that Jane Fonda had in the 1970s.

(796) Sadie is a fan of the actress Julia Garner.

(797) Sadie is a fan of strawberries.

(798) The Duffer Brothers got an awful lot of rejections when they first tried to pitch Stranger Things to television and

streaming companies. All told, they estimate that over a dozen people turned them down before a deal was struck with Netflix. There were a number of factors in why Stranger Things was so difficult to sell. The first problem was the fact that the Duffers were barely known and had little to no clout in Hollywood. They had previously made a horror film called Hidden which sat in mothballs for two years and was then a financial disaster when it got a limited release. They had also worked as writers on the first season of the television show Wayward Pines. While the first season of that show was watchable enough it was hardly the sort of thing to launch writers into superstardom. The third stumbling block for the Duffers was that they wanted a gang of kids to be the main characters in their show and the television and streaming executives they spoke to thought this was a stupid idea doomed to failure.

(799) In the scenes in Stranger Things where the characters are talking on walkie-talkies, the dialogue coming through the walkie-talkies is spoken to the actor on the set so they can react in a natural way.

(800) Max and Eleven are reading Tiger Beat Magazine in Eleven's bedroom in the Stranger Things 3 episode The Case of the Missing Lifeguard. Tiger Beat was a teen magazine for girls

(801) Sadie said she likes the high-waisted pants fashion of the 1980s.

(802) Sadie has expressed interest in exploring different film genres and taking on diverse roles in the future.

(803) One of the Netflix sound stages caught fire during the production of Stranger Things 4. Thankfully, no one was

injured.

(804) Sadie was very into Harry Potter when she was younger.

(805) Sadie said she made no plans for her 21st birthday and did not make a big fuss about it.

(806) Sadie said she broke or dropped so many Walkmans shooting Stranger Things 4 that in the end the props department made a fake Styrofoam one for Max to carry!

(807) Sadie said it was slightly tough to get into the swing of things on Stranger Things 2 because the cast all had a rapport with one another and she was the new kid.

(808) Sadie said she doesn't like parties - even on her birthday.

(809) You can, believe it or not, now buy candy made to look like Stranger Things 3 fertiliser.

(810) Sadie said she is a difficult person to buy a gift for because she can never think of anything she wants.

(811) A board game based on Stranger Things 'Christmas Ouija' sequences was released by Hasbro! The blurb for 'Ouija Stranger Things Game' is as follows: 'Gather around the Ouija: Stranger Things Edition game, if you dare, and unlock secrets from a mysterious and mystifying world of the Upside Down. Inspired by the Netflix Original Series, Stranger Things, this game board features the alphabet spelled out with Christmas lights like in the iconic light wall scene from the show (board does not light up). Summon the courage to ask the Ouija board questions about what happened in the Upside Down, as well as anything else you'd like to know. Will the planchette spell

out the answers that you seek? Handle the Ouija board with respect, and it won't disappoint you!'

(812) Sadie said most of her siblings have red hair too.

(813) Sadie has a Peloton exercise bike.

(814) Sadie said she was the only girl at school with red hair.

(815) Sadie said that when she was a kid she didn't know anything about fashion designers or brands.

(816) At the start of Stranger Things 2, Dustin fails to get the princess when he plays Dragon's Lair. This foreshadows the fact that he won't win the heart of Max. Dragon's Lair was an unusual game that came out in 1983. It featured animation by a former Disney animator named Don Bluth and was more of a choose your fate adventure than an arcade game. The player made a choice and then watched the next animation play out to see if they had made the right choice or the wrong choice. Dragon's Lair was popular at first but this type of game didn't catch on. Watching the game's hero Dirk the Daring get killed in cartoon animation simply became annoying (and expensive) for players. Even if you eventually worked out the pattern of choices to beat the game you'd have little motivation to return to it again. The animation you see when Dustin is playing the game is not actual 'gameplay' but the promo reel Dragon's Lair used to promote the game before it came out.

The Duffers personally disliked Dragon's Lair as a game but they thought the animation would be cool to have in an episode of Stranger Things. It would have cost around $4,000 to buy a Dragon's Lair arcade machine in 1984.

(817) Sadie said that a key reason why she stopped eating meat was a time as kid when she was in a buffet and there was a whole roasted pig on one of the tables - which she found 'gross'. Sadie made the connection between 'meat' and the fact that an innocent animal has to die to supply this meat. Thereafter she never ate meat again.

(818) Sadie says that Gaten Matarazzo is the worst culprit for making her laugh during a take on Stranger Things.

(819) Not only had Sadie not seen any Brendan Fraser films before she made The Whale but she'd never even heard of Brendan Fraser!

(820) Pac-Man was the most popular machine among the Stranger Things crew when they played the games in the Palace Arcade set.

(821) CCTV style footage named Hawkins Monitored was released to promote Stranger Things 2 in which you could secretly watch characters from the show.

(822) Sadie said it was unavoidably a bit strange to grow up in the public eye.

(823) Stranger Things 2 began production with a secret codename because the media and fans were so rabid for spoilers after the amazing success of season one.

(824) Sadie says she likes sport but isn't very co-ordinated or athletic.

(825) Sadie says she doesn't worry about fashion blunders.

(826) Sadie said she binged the first season of Stranger Things

inside two days. Little did she know she would end up in the show.

(827) Sadie says a ChapStick is an essential item for her.

(828) In 2017, a Stranger Things computer game was made by by Texas studio BonusXP, Inc. and published by Netflix. The game was free on the App Store and Google Play. The game is appropriately retro both in graphics and music to make it look like a video game from the eighties. The blurb went like this: 'Add characters to your party. Solve puzzles using their unique abilities. Lucas can nail things from afar with his Wrist Rocket. Nancy has a whole bag of bats to swing. Punch your way to answers with Hopper, who's also not afraid to don his dashing yellow hazmat suit for a little Upside Down action. Born after 1984? You might want to start with Normal difficulty, which lets you explore at your own pace. Death isn't even that bad. However, if you've honed your skills on the unforgiving games of yesteryear, then Classic is the soul-crushing mode for you. Completionist? Collect all the Eggos and Gnomes. Complete the full VHS library. Check off all the achievements. Who knows what secret characters or exclusive, never-before-seen-footage of Season 2 they might unlock...'

(829) Sadie said she feels more comfortable in her own skin now than she did when she was a young teenager.

(830) The comics we Eleven and Max looking at in Stranger Things 3 are issues 326 of Wonder Woman and 185 of Green Lantern. In issue 326 of Wonder Woman, Wonder Woman follows Keith Griggs and Lauren Haley to the Central American nation of Tropidor on an investigative mission, and again encounters Tezcatlipoca.

(831) The Ranker website voted the Stranger Things Back to the 90s Trivial Pursuit as the best board game inspired by the show.

(832) Sadie said she is sometimes a trifle wistful about the fact that her acting career meant she could never be a normal teenager.

(833) Video game fans think that Stranger Things 3 may have been influenced by Parasite Eve, a classic PS1-era RPG based on the novel by Hideaki Sena. Rats play a big part in the game.

(834) Sadie said that when she got the part of Annie on the stage her parents got her an Annie themed cookie cake to celebrate.

(835) The scenes of the kids hiding from the monster in Starcourt Mall in Stranger Things 3 have some obvious similarities to the children trying to hide from the raptors in Jurassic Park.

(836) Sadie believes that she has barely scratched the surface of what she can do as an actor.

(837) You can see breakfast cereals for Ghostbusters, Pac-Man, Donkey Kong, and Mr T in Stranger Things 3. These were all real cereals in 1985.

(838) Because of child labour laws, Sadie had to have a family guardian on the set of Stranger Things until she turned eighteen.

(839) The fairground scenes in Stranger Things 3 were shot in September. The cast found it a very chilly experience because it was getting cold but they (obviously) had to wear summer

clothes.

(840) Sadie said she found having to go to awards ceremonies a bit 'terrifying' when she joined the cast of Stranger Things.

(841) The film that is interrupted by the power cut in the Starcourt Mall in Suzie, Do You Copy? is George Romero's Day of the Dead. Day of the Dead was the third film in Romero's classic (original) zombie trilogy, following on from Night of the Living Dead and Dawn of the Dead (which, like much of Stranger Things 3, takes place in a huge shopping mall). Day of the Dead only got a wide release on July 19, 1985, so the Stranger Things kids must be attending a special preview. It's little wonder that Steve had to smuggle the kids in as Day of the Dead (which was unrated in the United States) is a famously gory film thanks to Tom Savini's wonderfully gruesome special effects.

(842) Sadie has done photo shoots for TopShop.

(843) The endless Stranger Things stuff you can now buy includes a Demogorgon dog hat (!), a Where's Barb? book, a Castle Byers snow globe, an Eggo Crossbody Bag, a Demogorgan Baby Bonnet, a Waffle Purse, and a Demogorgon Candle.

(844) Sadie said she never makes any plans or looks ahead and prefers to just go with the flow.

(845) The scene where Max and the kids push Dustin's radio tower aloft in Suzie, Do You Copy? seems to ape the famous World War 2 photograph where six United States Marines raised the flag atop Mount Suribachi at the Battle of Iwo Jima.

(846) Sadie says that musical theatre was like her 'acting boot

camp' and taught her a lot.

(847) Despite the abundance of rats in Stranger Things 3, a real rat was never used on the set.

(848) When Sadie was working on the stage as a kid she said she and the other kids would put on little backstage productions purely for fun.

(849) Canada was the country where the first season of Stranger Things went viral the fastest.

(850) Sadie said that shooting the battle between Billy and the kids in The Sauna Test was the most exhausting time she had on the set in Stranger Things 3.

(851) According to Parrot Analytics, over the four-day period of its initial release, Stranger Things 3 registered 3.2 times the 'demand expressions' of Game of Thrones.

(852) When they first started casting for Max in Stranger Things 2, the Duffers made the mistake of testing girls who were too young. They had forgotten that the kids from season one were somewhat older and taller now.

(853) Sadie is a fan of the musical Wicked. Wicked is a popular musical that is based on the novel "Wicked: The Life and Times of the Wicked Witch of the West" by Gregory Maguire.

(854) Vecna's lair (which is officially known as his Mindscape and a place that Max barely escaped from) and Henry Creel's first wander through the terrifying (not that Henry finds it terrifying - he seems to love the place!) Upside Down in Stranger Things 4 was partly inspired by some of the bleaker work of the German painter Caspar David Friedrich. Friedrich,

who died in 1840, was known for depicting solitary figures in lonely landscapes.

(855) Sadie says she knows all the words to High School Musical.

(856) Sadie said she is proud to be a 'theatre dork'.

(857) Stranger Things merch has, not surprisingly, exploded with the immense popularity of the show around the world. What is though the most valuable Stranger Things item on the market? Well, it to be a Hopper Gold Funko autographed by David Harbour. This is valued at $6,500.

(858) Sadie said her career stalled around 2016 because she was too old for child actor parts and too young for adult roles. As a consequence she went back to school because she couldn't get any work. Luckily though Stranger Things just was around the corner.

(859) Stranger Things 4 breaks with tradition in that it is the only season of the show where the groups of characters do not all meet up and work together at the end.

(860) Sadie's family live in Summit. Summit is a commuter town in New Jersey and has a population of about 22,000. Meryl Streep was born in Summit.

(861) Stranger Things never really pinpoints where exactly in Indiana the town of Hawkins is located. One of the spin-off novels seems to place it near Bloomington.

(862) Sadie has been to Milan fashion week.

(863) Hallmark's Keepsake Ornament collection for the 2020

holiday season included a Demogorgon ornament designed for your Christmas tree.

(864) Sadie has done promotion for Nike.

(865) The first teaser trailer for Stranger Things 2 featured a real 1980 Eggo commercial featuring Wonder Years star Jason Hervey.

(866) Sadie is partial to a bucket hat.

(867) In the employee room of the Palace Arcade in Stranger Things 2 you can see posters for Q*bert and Crystal Castles.

(868) Sadie said that she never quite feels like herself when she dressed in designer clothes for some swanky premiere.

(869) The Stranger Things YouTube channel receives about ten million views a month.

(870) Sadie seems to be fond of wearing blazers.

(871) The success of Stranger Things has been very important to Netflix because it has essentially given the platform their first franchise. Stranger Things had little merch or promotion in its first season but now Stranger Things merch is all over the place and there have been video games, commercial deals with brands like Cocoa-Cola and Nike, and even talk of Stranger Things spin-off shows when the series ends. It seems inevitable that Netflix will not want the Stranger Things brand to lay dormant when the show ends and be looking for ways to bring it back in some form or other.

(872) Sadie said that she and her siblings were not allowed to watch too many films or TV shows growing-up. They were

encouraged to read or be active.

(873) Sadie attended the Toronto International Film Festival in 2022.

(874) The only two of the kids in Stranger Things who never met Dr Brenner in the show are Will Byers and Max.

(875) Sadie visited Prague when she had some time off. She said she loves European castles.

(876) Sadie said that a quiet dinner somewhere is her idea of a good night out.

(877) When the kids are under siege in the Gap store in the season finale of Stranger Things 3, there are camera shots designed to mimic Steven Spielberg's adaptation of The War of the Worlds. The scene that Stranger Things 3 riffs on is that of Tom Cruise and Dakota Fanning trapped in a basement trying to evade alien probes.

(878) We see the characters drinking 'New Coke' in Stranger Things 3 - although opinion is mixed. Lucas seems to like it but his friends don't. In 1985, Coca-Cola was rebranded as "New Coke" and Americans were up in arms. The company quickly received 40,000 letters and phone calls demanding that the original Coke be brought back. There were protest groups formed to demand the return of the old Coke and - eventually - the original was released again in parallel with New Coke.

(879) Sadie is a fan of the Aesop skin cleanser.

(880) Sadie wore an Alexander McQueen dress to the Venice Film festival.

(881) Why does Eleven snub Max in the finale of Stranger Things 2? Sadie offered her own explanation - "Well, Eleven hasn't met many girls her own age before, so when she saw Max she immediately saw her as a threat."

(882) Sadie said that red carpet events are not nearly as glamorous as they look on television.

(883) Sadie is a fan of the musical Hairspray.

(884) Sadie thinks that becoming a vegan is quite easy now with the extensive range of vegan food and drinks you can buy.

(885) Sadie said she changes her fragrance quite often to 'mix up' her smell.

(886) Sadie said she loves the smell of nail salons!

(887) The Fear Street films were directed by Leigh Janiak. Leigh Janiak is the wife of Ross Duffer - one of the co-creators of Stranger Things.

(888) When Stranger Things 2 was due for release, a man named Harry Moore made a contract for his girlfriend to sign so that he could avoid spoilers! The contract said - "no episode of Stranger Things Series Two to be consumed in the absence of your partner, all spoilers to be avoided, in the event of a spoiler being discovered it must not be shared with your partner, neither partner may be in the same room as 'Stranger Things Series Two' episode unless with your partner, series one episodes are excluded from this contract."

(889) Stranger Things 4 began shooting in February 2020 but production was then halted for several months because of the

pandemic. Sadie said that some scenes in that season were shot over a year apart!

(890) Sadie says that Taylor Swift has become something of a mentor to her.

(891) In 2018, Sadie made her runway debut for designer Jun Takahashi.

(892) Sadie said that To Kill a Mockingbird is one of her favourite books.

(893) Sadie said she watched the Disney channel a lot when she was a kid.

(894) Sadie said the thought of acting and performing on the stage in front of an audience is a slightly scary thought now because she hasn't done it for a long time.

(896) Sadie says she doesn't like her eyebrows to be too thin.

(897) Sadie is a fan of Audrey Hepburn.

(898) The bright raincoats that Eleven and Max wear in The Case of the Missing Lifeguard evoke many films - including Don't Look Now, The Shining, David Cronenberg's The Brood, and Friday the 13th.

(899) The Duffer Brothers say they like to have a couple of new characters in each season of Stranger Things because it shakes things up a bit and adds a fresh dynamic to the show.

(900) There was a slight battle between Netflix and the Duffers on Stranger Things 2 when it came to swearing. Netflix wanted to do alternative takes of the scenes where the kids

swear so that bad language was almost non existent. The kids hated this idea because they thought scenes were much funnier with a few stray cuss words by their characters. The Duffers liked the takes with the cuss words too so in the end Netflix conceded and allowed the occasional swear word.

(901) You see some Crush orange drinks in Stranger Things 3. Crush is a brand of carbonated soft drinks owned and marketed internationally by Keurig Dr Pepper, originally created as an orange soda. Crush mainly competes with Coca-Cola's Fanta. It was created in 1911 by beverage and extract chemist Neil C. Ward.

(902) Some of the overhead camera shots of the rain in Stranger Things 3 (during the storm) mimic shots David Fincher used in his 1995 film Seven.

(903) Sadie is not a 'nepo baby' or Disney factory kid. She has become famous under her own steam.

(904) The only game Sadie said she understood and liked shooting the arcade scenes in Stranger Things 2 was Pac-Man. Pac-Man was estimated to have had 30 million active players across the United States in the early 1980s.

(905) You can now, should you desire, buy some glow in the dark Stranger Things sneakers.

(906) Sadie said that if she could have one superpower it would be the ability to teleport anywhere. Sadie said she would love to be able to read minds!

(907) Sadie is a fan of the 90s music group TLC.

(908) Sadie said that Urban Outfitters is one of her favourite

places to browse online.

(909) Sadie said her favourite skincare product is May Lindstrom's The Blue Cocoon.

(910) Sadie said she had always planned to go college but the pandemic made her rethink those plans.

(911) Sadie bought herself a Tesla car on her 18th birthday.

(912) Sadie is said to own four cars in all - though she apparently doesn't use them much.

(913) Sadie said she could drive at one point but doesn't drive anymore.

(914) H.P Lovecraft was an inspiration for Stranger Things. Lovecraft was a horror author who imagined a universe full of inexplicable creatures, dimensions and entities that can't be explained.

(915) Sadie has been involved in anti-bullying campaigns.

(916) Sadie said that when you come off a big film or TV project (like Stranger Things) it is difficult to get back into a normal routine and normal sleep patterns again.

(917) Sadie that her favorite episode of Stranger Things 3 is The Spy.

(918) Sadie says she often tends to heat up ready meals at home.

(919) The watch worn by Max in season two of Stranger Things is a Swatch Yellow Racer.

(920) Max appears to have a crush on Ralph Macchio from The Karate Kid in Stranger Things 3. The Karate Kid was released in 1984. There were two Karate Kid sequels (with Ralph Macchio) in 1986 and 1989. An attempt to reboot the franchise with The Next Karate Kid in 1994 didn't work. In the 1994 film, Hilary Swank (in only her second film role) became the new 'karate kid'.

(921) Sadie has attended New York Giants games. This is an American football team.

(922) Sadie made her Broadway debut at the age of eleven in the play Annie where she played the role of Duffy.

(923) Saidie said her kiss with Caleb McLaughlin in Stranger Things 2 was deeply weird because it took place in front of 200 extras and her mother!

(924) Sadie said she likes working with the Duffer Brothers on Stranger Things because they "aren't very strict" as directors.

(925) Dustin's 'totally tubular' catchphrase in Stranger Things 2 is because Max is from California. The specific source is Frank Zappa's 1982 Valley Girl single.

(926) Sadie's favourite episode of Seinfeld is called The Parking Garage.

(927) Sadie went to a cheerleading camp when she was younger.

(928) Sadie is a big fan of the musical film Grease.

(929) Sadie is a fan of arugula smoothies.

(930) When Billy is in his car and threatens to run the boys over in Stranger Things 2 he asks Max if he'll get earn 'points' for hitting them all at once. This is a reference to the 1975 movie Death Race 2000. In that film a dystopian future has a violent car race where you get points for running over pedestrians.

(931) The Stranger Things opening title sequence is constructed to look like a cryptic puzzle that is slowly revealing itself.

(932) Sadie said that Love is Blind was her 'guilty pleasure' TV show. This was a dating reality show.

(933) Sadie said she loved the Hunger Games books growing up.

(934) There is a sly costume Easter egg near the end of Stranger Things 3 when Lucas and Max wear outfits worn by Eric and Donna in 'That 70s Show.

(935) Sadie and the children in the cast of Stranger Things 2 had to arrange their schooling around filming and were assigned tutors and a classroom on the set.

(936) Sadie has a fear of snakes.

(937) Sadie is a fan of the band Daft Punk.

(938) Sadie's favourite Taylor Swift song is (no surprise here) All Too Well.

(939) Patrick Henry High School, used as the school in Stranger Things, closed as a real school in 2015 because the building had a problem with mould.

(940) Sadie said that Broadway is surprisingly obstreperous because you have all these child actors running around screaming and singing!

(941) Sadie is a fan of Zac Efron.

(942) Stranger Things 4 definitely got a slight backlash from some hardcore lifelong Kate Bush fans. Some of these fans seemed a trifle irritated and snooty about the fact that many young people only became aware of Kate Bush through a popular television show! Kate Bush certainly wasn't complaining though. She seemed very touched and happy that one of her songs had been chosen to play such a pivotal role in the show.

(943) The place where Sadie and Millie Bobby Brown went on holiday together after shooting Stranger Things 2 was Cabo San Lucas, Mexico.

(944) Sadie said it was a bit weird when she got a Stranger Things 2 audition because only a few days before she had binged the first season.

(945) The Stranger Things kids watched the Superbowl teaser for Stranger Things 2 together and got quite excited.

(946) Sadie said that it was easier to do kissing scenes with Caleb McLaughlin because they knew each somewhat from their stage days in New York.

(947) Sadie said she hates not working for too long and prefers to keep busy.

(948) Propmaster Linda Reiss says that the Michael Myers mask that Max wears on Halloween night in Stranger Things 2

had to look as if Max had made it herself because you couldn't buy a Michael Myers mask in 1984. "The actual Michael Myers mask was not on sale at the time of our show in 1984, so we had to make it look like Max had done what the Halloween prop people did: Take a Shatner (Star Trek) mask and paint it. We took a Myers mask that was the style used in the first movie, and removed a bunch of paint so it had the feel of a flesh-colored mask that had been painted."

(949) Sadie said her best female friend is someone she has known since school.

(950) In Stranger Things 2, Lucas chooses to tell Max about the fantastical and frightening events that happened in Hawkins the previous year. Of course, she doesn't believe him at first. Max complains that Lucas isn't very original with his tale of alternate dimensions and monsters. This is the Duffers having a joke at their own expense. When you find a criticism of Stranger Things it is usually someone complaining that the show isn't very original (a view which appears to completely miss the point of Stranger things).

(951) There are a number of Indiana Jones and the Temple of Doom references in Stranger Things 2. The scene where Max can't reach the pedals on the car so has to improvise was based on a similar scene with Short Round in Temple of Doom.

(952) Sadie has appeared on the cover of Seventeen magazine.

(953) Sadie has expressed an interest in working on more independent films.

(954) Lucy Lu's Coffee Cafe in Jackson created a Stranger Drinks menu in 2017. The most popular choices were 'Sheriff

Hopper', a hazelnut and vanilla coffee drink, and the 'Demogorgon', a frappe with blood-red food colouring

(955) Sadie says she was overwhelmed when she learned she'd won the part of Max. "I was at school at my speaking debate practice and my mom texted me and was like, "Get in the car right now" and she was like, "No I don't care you need to get in the car." So I knew something was off. I was like, "Why do you need me in the car so fast?" and she said, "I need to take your sister to a play date!" and I was really confused. So then I started to put everything together and realized that I must have been getting a call from the director soon to tell me I got the part. Sure enough, when I got home the phone rang and my mom handed it to me and they told me I got it. I didn't really know how to process it."

(956) Sadie enjoys drawing in her spare time.

(957) Sadie said her friends sometimes ask her for fashion advice.

(958) Sadie described life on the set of Stranger Things as like being at summer camp.

(959) Sadie is a fan of music festivals.

(960) Sadie said it will be 'terrible' when Stranger Things ends because the cast and crew are like family.

(961) Sadie said she will miss the 'acting security' of Stranger Things. That feeling of knowing you have a guaranteed job to go back to.

(962) Sadie said she was originally rejected for the part of Max because she was deemed too old. She begged for a chance to

read again though and eventually won them over.

(963) Sadie said that she thinks most young people enjoy social media much more than she does.

(964) Sadie was amazed by Starcourt Mall set in Stranger Things 3. "Every single store was decked out with things that would actually be in that store in 1985. Wicks 'N' Sticks had about 1,000 old-school candles. My favourite place was the shoe store, where El tried to walk in heels and fell. It had all of these crazy vintage shoes, like sneakers that are worth thousands of dollars now. We were given strict instructions - Do not touch the Nikes! These are on loan!"

(965) Gaten Matarazzo said it was a great relief to him that the Kate Bush song Running Up That Hill became a big deal in Stranger Things 4 because people finally stopped going on about the Neverending Story song he had to sing in season three!

(966) Sadie said her favourite subject at school was maths.

(967) The Snow Ball scenes in Stranger Things 2 took two days to shoot.

(968) In 2018 and 2020, Sadie was nominated for the MTV Movie & TV Awards and Screen Actors Guild Awards for outstanding performance in Stranger Things.

(969) Sadie said she told a bit of a fib at her Stranger Things audition and pretended she was good at rollerblading.

(970) Sadie wore a Chanel Cashmere Pullover on The Kelly Clarkson Show.

(971) Sadie is a fan of the Roberto Benigni film Life is Beautiful.

(972) The younger cast members in Stranger Things like to decorate their trailers when a new season is in production.

(973) Sadie said she loves artichokes.

(974) The strange and secret scientific intrigue in Stranger Things was partly inspired by conspiracy theories concerning the real life Montauk Air Force Station. The base was closed down in the 1980s but this decaying site - still dominated by an imposing and ghostly radar antenna - was later the source for all manner of outlandish conspiracy theories involving kidnapped children, LSD experiments, monsters, teleportation, telekinesis, quantum fields, and time travel.

(975) Sadie says she loves to make butternut squash and spinach lasagna.

(976) The survey site YouGov reported that 10% of British Netflix subscribers binged the entire second season of Stranger Things in one day.

(977) Sadie first met Gaten Matarazzo and Caleb McLaughlin at a park in New York where all the Broadway kids would go to play between shows.

(978) According to entertainment sites, Sadie was paid $150,000 an episode on Stranger Things 3. This would have put her below the salary of the other teens in the show. Presumably this was because the others had been in the show longer than Sadie?

(979) Max and Eleven are like a pair of little detectives in the

Stranger Things 3 episode The Case of the Missing Lifeguard when they investigate Billy together. This amusingly (and unwittingly) anticipates the fact that Millie Bobby Brown would later play Enola Holmes.

(980) When we see Max and Eleven discover the body in the bath in Stranger Things 3, this seems a lot like a homage to a similar scene in the film adaptation of Stephen King's The Dead Zone.

(981) Sadie is a fan of the (defunct) pop group Oasis. Her favourite Oasis song is Wonderwall.

(982) The meat that Steve and Dustin use on the railway tracks and junkyard to attract Dart in Stranger Things 2 was in reality a mixture of watermelon and beef. Sadie didn't enjoy the scenes with the beef and watermelon because she's a vegan.

(983) Sadie said that one of her favourite films is The Devil Wears Prada.

(984) Loch Nora, where the kids go trick or treating in Stranger Things 2, is the name of a real place near where the Duffer Brothers grew up in North Carolina.

(985) Sadie likes green tea.

(986) Sadie said she likes fashion to have an 'edge' to it.

(987) In Stranger Things 2, you can hear a small burst of the music from Joe Dante's Gremlins when Dart escapes from the AV room.

(988) Sadie said that when it comes to shoes she goes for

comfort rather than what they look like.

(989) Sadie describes herself as a 'laid-back' person in real life.

(990) Sadie is a fan of Starbucks.

(991) Sadie says she never had a celebrity crush when she was growing-up.

(992) Sadie is a fan of the film La La Land.

(993) The Lovecraft story which has the most similarities with Stranger Things is From Beyond. The book was published in 1920 and is about dark secret dimensions unknown to man.

(994) Sadie said she lived alone for the first time in her life when she made The Whale. She said this helped her to get into character more.

(995) Sadie said of her Stranger Things audition - "I was like - if I don't get this, the world is going to end."

(996) Sadie says she has a unique bond with her young Stranger Things co-stars. "The bond that we have... you can't describe it. We've grown up together in this really unique situation and we've always had each other to lean on and talk to. We understand each other in a different way."

(997) Sadie said you have to shed those 'child actor habits' when you grow up and take on more mature roles - as she did in The Whale.

(998) Sadie is a fan of the Sì fragrance by Armani.

(999) Sadie's most treasured piece of clothing is a denim

jacket with fuzzy lining.

(1000) It is perfectly possible that Netflix might try and do a Stranger Things reunion special one day in the future so Stranger Things 5 might not necessarily be the end for Sadie and Max!

Photo Credit

14 July 2018

https://commons.wikimedia.org/wiki/File:Sadie_Sink_2-00362_%2843866090832%29_%28cropped%29.jpg

Super Festivals